SCOTLAND

FROM THE AIR

FOREWORD

UNTIL THE EARLY TWENTIETH CENTURY, shepherds and foresters perhaps had viewed Scotland from heights, and these no higher than mountain slopes. Shepherds and foresters didn't climb up there for the view, but in order to do their jobs. It was the Romantics who saw grandeur and sublimity in heights. Keats climbed Ben Nevis; Byron wrote about 'dark Lochnagar'.

The Vikings from Norway saw Scotland from the sea: a flat poor place Rinansay in Orkney, for example, must have seemed to their level hawk-eyes. The peasants of the Lowlands and the western fringes saw monotonies of back-breaking tilth and pasture: Burns, the most inspired of them, was more intrigued by his fellow men and women than by landscape; he hardly mentions the sea at all; but 'trotting burns' were akin to his heart's lyric measures.

Then the Wright brothers strung together the first aeroplane, and all was changed. Men could look down on the land and sea, mountain and firth, city and village and river, 'as the hawk sees it or the helmeted airman'. A Scottish pilot, the Duke of Hamilton, was the first to fly over Mount Everest. An astronaut with a Scottish name, Armstrong, was the first earthling to step on to the moon; and from there look back on the blue-and-silver of the mother planet.

It is true that the eighteenth-century balloonists, Tytler and Lunardi, had drifted high over Scotland. And now, in 1984, there's hardly a Scots person who hasn't looked down from the sonorous height of a plane on the snow-veined Grampians, on the oil-and-fish-rich sea, on the storied northern islands and the lyrical melancholy islands of the west, on Edinburgh castle and the shipyards of Glasgow, on scattered lochs and glinting rivers, on the fertile reaches of the Mearns and the gentle hills of the Borders that begot the greatest ballads in the world. Scotland is truly a beautiful country, with extraordinary variety.

What strikes the traveller who has taken the hawk's-path for the first time is the extraordinary neatness and cleanness of all the goings-on below: the sheep and cows are in their places in neat squared fields; cars move with precision on the little clean ribbon-like roads, as if impelled by some kindly Fate (for up here the noises, frustrations and fumes are cancelled); and the rivers are 'grave mighty thoughts threading a dream'.

The imagination of Edwin Muir, the great modern Scottish poet (who, I seem to remember, was rarely if ever airborne in his life), caught the purity and timelessness of it, as the gods reclined on their mountain-isle summits.

> While down below the little ships sailed by,
> Toy multitudes swarmed in the harbours, shepherds drove
> Their tiny flocks to the pastures, marriage feasts
> Went on below, small birthdays and holidays,

Ploughing and harvesting and life and death.
And all permissible, all acceptable,
Clear and secure as in a limpid dream. . . .

So, to the good cloud-borne photographer as to the poet, the turbulent history, the gray present, and the uncertain future of Scotland are seen in a perspective of tranquil enduring things.

George Mackay Brown
January 1984

INTRODUCTION

MAINLAND SCOTLAND is roughly three-fifths of the size of England and contains about one-tenth of Britain's total population of fifty-five million. The majority of Scots live in the Lowland triangle defined by Glasgow to the west, Stirling to the north and Edinburgh to the east. A small country, then, with an even smaller one set within it. But to the traveller in Scotland profound differences – in people and their speech, in landscape, in weather – are apparent as he moves from coast to coast or even from one town to another. There are also almost 700 islands scattered at all points around the Scottish coastline, each distinct from the others in natural features and, where inhabited, in custom.

In *Scotland from the Air* we have appropriated the miraculous machine which has reduced to almost nothing that part of travel once thought to be the best – the journey – and combined it with the camera to make a new kind of tour. 150 pictures follow which have been selected from the archives of Aerofilms Library. Founded in 1919, the company holds a collection of over 800,000 views which is continually updated and constitutes an unusual historical record as well as, more obviously, an important geographical one. Starting near the eastern border with England, we take an anti-clockwise route north, arriving back at Berwick. The photographs lead us along what George Mackay Brown calls 'the hawk's-path', sustaining throughout that perspective which normally is only glimpsed at the giddy moments of take-off and landing during an aeroplane flight. They show, simultaneously, the landscape's multifariousness and its curious order.

The photographs in *Scotland from the Air* are a lavish entertainment, but they also add up to an intriguing document. An aerial photograph is capable of showing several stages in the development of a town or city all at once. In the same way, the process by which an island or a mountain achieved its shape is slightly more comprehensible when it is viewed from above; the path of a river criss-crosses its own ancient cast-off routes; the complexity of a harbour suggests past vitality as much as it reveals present redundancy. This camera sees not only the castles and lochs by which (bonnie) Scotland is popularly recognized, but also the industrial sites which are essential to its sustenance, not forgetting the quarries and canals which used to be.

Some of the images, such as that of Loch Avon (page 57), have not altered in 10,000 years (though very few have ever seen it like this); others, like Hillington industrial estate (p. 137) and Cumbernauld new town (p. 140), are entirely twentieth-century creations; yet others, such as Lochan Shira (p. 105) with its hydro-electric dam, are a mixture of antiquity and modernity – in this case with aesthetically pleasing results. At first glance Lochan Shira could be mistaken for an abstract painting, but other pictures are more subtly deceptive: the landscape around Loch Choire in Sutherland (p. 83), for example, only 180 years ago would have been busy with the activity of crofters, perhaps even a small township. However, almost all inland townships in this county were emptied and demolished during the events known as the Highland Clearances.

Occasionally, multiple layers of Scottish history are revealed in a single image. The Eildon Hills in

Roxburgh (p. 17), for example, are today renowned as the beauty spot associated with Sir Walter Scott. But an aerial view shows clearly the pattern of a Pictish hilltop town, which was in turn superseded by a Roman lookout post. Snug below the main hill is the town of Melrose and its medieval abbey. Or, again, in the photograph of Ullapool (p. 91), the purposeful beginnings of the town as a fishing station are starkly apparent in its gridiron layout, and the viewer's fascination rests partly in recognizing both how much and how little the modern resort has departed from the original.

One of the things I like most about these photographs is that the aerial perspective makes it hard for the camera to deceive. By seeing only what it wants to the camera almost always lies; but its deceptions are more difficult to carry out while it is several hundred feet aloft. For that reason, the pictures in this book do not pretend – as so many photographic collections do – that Scotland can be viewed simply. That is to the good, for the country is notoriously prone to the kind of beguiling romance which transforms history into nostalgia.

Scotland from the ground sometimes seems like a set of conundrums: an ancient nation which is no longer a state; proud of its clerical, legal and educational systems but lacking a government; begetter of many famous sons which for centuries has watched its children leave in droves; confused about language but with a diverse literature written in three different ones; incorporating the most beautiful region in Europe which has been described by its own inhabitants as a wasteland . . .

And so on and so on. Yet Scotland endures this tragi-comic muddle. As with some of the small islands you are about to pass over – Fidra (p. 22) and Inchcolm (p. 33) are only two examples – the richness of this nation's history is out of proportion to its size; and in past achievements rest future possibilities. *Scotland from the Air* makes no effort to avoid these paradoxes; if it did, then the camera would certainly be guilty of lying.

A genuine list of sources would include everything from the pages of the daily *Scotsman* to all three sets of the multi-volume *Statistical Account of Scotland*, first published in the late eighteenth century. In addition to those, and much else besides, I have found particularly helpful the compendious gazetteer in Moray McLaren's *Shell Guide to Scotland* (1965).

Iain Crichton Smith's poem 'Johnson in the Highlands' comes from *The Law and the Grace* (1965); Hugh MacDiarmid's essay 'Growing Up in Langholm' was published in *Memoirs of a Modern Scotland* edited by Karl Miller (1970).

To Alan Taylor of Edinburgh Central Libraries, Michael Mellor, my editor Barbara Mellor, and Hilary Davies, I owe special thanks.

Langside Burn and Maiden Paps, Roxburgh, Borders

Many travellers in Scotland would choose the Borders if asked to state their first preference in Scottish landscape (though it would be an unfair demand). Borders scenery is calmer, greener, more reassuring than the imposing Highland glens which by virtue of their photogenic nature have come to represent the essential Scotland. The smaller hills east of the Cheviots — one of two natural frontiers which divide Scotland from England, the other being the River Tweed — give rise to numerous burns which trickle sometimes for many miles, often just a few hundred yards, before feeding greater streams. From somewhere deep in the Maiden Paps (*right*, 1677 feet high and christened by a more playful generation) the Harwood Burn springs, is drawn into the Langside Burn (*left*) and eventually reaches the River Teviot at Hawick, though not before undergoing a few more transformations. In this picture, facing north, it looks like a piece of string left to lie as it falls, but as the oxbow bends testify, it has not settled for its present course without a great deal of serpentine deliberation.

10

◁ **Kelso**, Roxburgh, Borders

Known in the Middle Ages as 'Chalkou', chalk hill, Kelso is today a compact market town situated, like others in the Borders (the main centres besides this are Melrose, Galashiels, Selkirk and Hawick), so as to combine the advantages of town and country: ten minutes' walk from the spacious Georgian square in the dead centre of our picture takes you into fresh countryside. The county town in medieval times was Roxburgh, but owing to its position on the north bank of the Tweed, near the confluence of that river with the Teviot, Kelso grew in importance and prosperity over the centuries without sacrificing its simplicity. Gas was introduced into Scotland here in 1818, at a coppersmith's shop in Bridge Street.

Kelso Abbey ▷

The small tidy ruin, pleasantly situated at the centre of Kelso, is the remnant of what was probably the greatest of all Border abbeys. For a long time it was assumed that the living body had fitted the skeleton, and that Kelso Abbey was a minor affair, but what you see here is now thought to be only the west end. Like other Border towns, Kelso has suffered countless English transgressions and one of those, in 1545, brought the life of its abbey to a close. Afterwards, the transept was used as a parish church, but that came to an end too, in the eighteenth century, when the roof fell in. Fortunately the faithful were elsewhere.

Dryburgh Abbey, Berwickshire, Borders ▽

When William and Dorothy Wordsworth visited Dryburgh in 1803 during their tour of Scotland (recorded by Dorothy) they were admitted to the abbey by a goblin-like woman who smelled of peat: 'If she had emitted smoke by her breath and through every pore, the odour could not have been stronger', wrote the poet's sister. The abbey itself proved to be adequate compensation, however. Dryburgh is one of a group of Border monasteries founded during the twelfth century, and it originally housed Northumbrian monks. It is the most peaceful, because the most remote, of all the monasteries in the Borders, and its claustral buildings set among trees and lawns are in a more complete state than any other on the Scottish mainland. They give strong aid to the imagination which wishes to reconstruct a picture of medieval monastic life. Dryburgh Abbey was destroyed by the English several times before the final blow in 1544. Walter Scott, to his everlasting content, was permitted to 'stretch his bones' here.

Floors Castle, Roxburgh, Borders ▷

The village of Roxburgh as it exists today is barely noticeable, as it quietly gets on with its farming business by the banks of the River Teviot in the Borders heartland. But in the Middle Ages there was a town of the same name about a mile away (to which the village provided relief for overcrowding), which was of great importance as one of the nation's four royal burghs. Its castle, a royal residence, is visible now only as an earthwork and a few stones on the river to the south of Kelso. It fell into English hands on several occasions, as the border was tossed before and behind it, and became fixed in Scotland only in 1460. The present Duke of Roxburghe has his seat in this mansion, with 55,000 green acres around it. It was designed by Vanburgh, built in 1725 by William Adam and augmented by Playfair in the middle of the nineteenth century.

It springs out of the ground in Tweedsmuir in the Southern Uplands, then trickles and flows to nourish ninety-seven miles of Borders country before surrendering to the sea at Berwick. For its last two miles the Tweed has an English voice. So much in Borders history depends on this river, not least the development of several of the main towns: Kelso, Galashiels and Melrose, all of which exploit its energy for industrial purposes, some of them to produce – tweed (although the name of the cloth does not derive from the river). Sir Walter Scott lived and died beside the Tweed, at Abbotsford, the mock medieval fantasy he built on its banks. Here, looking north, the disused railway viaduct (the Borders now possesses no railway system of its own) crosses beside the old and new bridges, near Newstead, a mile or so to the east of Melrose.

Eildon Hills, Roxburgh, Borders ▷

This area of the Borders is sometimes called Scott country, and the compact Eildon Hills (only one of three is in view here) are the central feature of the beauty spot known as Walter Scott's View. The hills are well served by legend. Beneath them Thomas the Rhymer spent seven years with the Faery Queen, who rewarded him with the gift of prophecy; here also it is said that King Arthur and his Knights lie in enchanted sleep; and in Melrose Abbey, just on the left of the road leading to the town from the river, is the supposed tomb of Michael Scot the wizard, who made the three peaks out of one. Scott the novelist thrived on such stories and even contributed to the lore himself. Perhaps the most frequently repeated anecdote concerns his horse, which stopped before the hills on its way to its master's funeral in Dryburgh Abbey, as had been its rider's habit. In the Bronze Age this northernmost summit was a hilltop town; look hard and you will see its remains. As many as a thousand people lived here. They were hostile to the Romans, naturally, who after their arrival in Tweeddale in AD 79 used the settlement as a signal station for the garrison at Trimontium, not far to the left along the Tweed.

△ **Bowhill,** Selkirkshire, Borders

The Yarrow and the Ettrick waters meet just a mile or so south-west of the town of Selkirk, and at their junction stands this rambling Georgian mansion, started by the 3rd Duke of Buccleuch in 1795 and worked on by several hands, including William Atkinson and William Burn. Until James v beat them out of it in the sixteenth century, the Ettrick Forest was a great tract of wooded land rich with game and thick with reivers and freebooters, some of whose exploits are recorded in the Border Ballads. Bowhill is open to the public, who come to see its collection of paintings, with works by Leonardo, Canaletto, Claude, Gainsborough and Reynolds,

and also relics of Scott, who was Sheriff of nearby Selkirk and who did so much to popularize and romanticize the region through his work (including that on the ballads).

Duns Castle, Berwickshire, Borders

The town of Duns, about a mile from the castle, has been the regent county town of Berwickshire since the town of Berwick ceased to be in Scotland. The little market town, which took its name from the 'dun' (hill) on which it is built and gave it to the medieval scholar Duns Scotus, has a population of less than two thousand. This

castle is a 'gothyck' pretender, built long after the days of seige by Gillespie Graham, on the site of an older building, part of which is incorporated into it. For turreted piles of this sort the designer typically chose a picturesque setting, and Duns is no exception. On the subject of famous men, it should be said in fairness that at least two other places claim Duns Scotus as their own, one of them in England and the other in Ireland. About Jim Clark the racing driver there is no squabbling, however; he was born here and was killed on the track (in Germany) in 1968; a small museum in town houses some of his trophies.

18

Tantallon, East Lothian, Lothian

Both road and rail north to Edinburgh from England run through country like this after crossing the border at Berwick. With sea and cliffs on one side and portions of sweet land on the other, no more beguiling introduction could be found. Then comes the sight of a Scottish castle. Tantallon (you must diverge slightly from the main road to reach it) has survived six centuries of military might, not to mention east-coast weather, better than most – giving rise to the expression to 'ding doon Tantallon Castle', meaning that such a destructive feat is tantamount to impossibility. The first Scottish castles, usually made of wood, were built by the Norman ruling class during the eleventh and twelfth centuries. These were followed by far more formidable houses, of which this is one of the best examples. Like others (for example, Mingary and Loch Leven) it is protected by a curtain wall, a non-load-bearing structure built to defy the sea and severe weather, which in this case is twelve feet thick in places. As for military security, Tantallon has a moat and towers on one side, and hundred-foot cliffs down to the sea on the others. It was a Douglas stronghold until it was conquered and dismantled during the Cromwellian occupation in 1651; but its rosy red sandstone, quarried locally, has remained in place since then.

△ Fidra, East Lothian, Lothian

Borrowston Rig, Berwickshire, Borders ▷

Fidra is one of a quartet of small volcanic rocks projecting from the Firth of Forth off the Lothian coast; the others are Lamb, Craigleith and Bass Rock. Together they contribute to the sense, when in the Lothians, of being close to country, sea and city. An extraordinary amount of activity has centred on this dot in the Forth through the ages: medieval remnants have been excavated from a cave, there are remains of a castle, and the reef which connects Fidra to the mainland has traces of a church. Nowadays it is the preserve of colonies of terns, and the naturalists who come to study their behaviour.

The stone circle at Borrowston Rig is one of a number of prehistoric monuments at that site in the Border parish of Lauder. If you are looking for stones, then look harder: none in this ring protrudes more than two feet above the earth. The purpose of such circles remains a mystery to us, apart from the likelihood that they were used by their builders in some form of sun worship. The mystery seems only to have been deepened when Borrowston was excavated some years ago and Bronze Age burial remains were found.

Livingston, West Lothian, Lothian

The M8 motorway was laid down in the 1970s to improve the notorious route between Edinburgh and Glasgow. No matter how many times you make the journey, the sensation remains of setting off in one country and stepping down in another, so different are the two cities' personalities. Before the advent of modern transport this disparity was partly explained by the length of time taken to reach one from the other, but nowadays the experience is still remarked upon. Fifteen miles west of Edinburgh the motorway passes through Livingston, a New Town begun in 1962. At the outset the target population for 1984 was 70,000; todays it stands at just over half that figure. As the picture suggests, a town for the motor car age. Here we look at the small industrial estate at Deans on Livingston's western fringe, with Bathgate up ahead.

Ingliston, Midlothian, Lothian ▷

Every year during the summer, farmers from all over the country make for Ingliston, six miles from Edinburgh, and the Royal Highland and Agricultural Society's Royal Highland Show. The Show used to come to them: from the 1820s the Society presented a circuit but the difficulty of obtaining decent temporary sites, often in small towns, finally drove it to look for a permanent home. In 1958 it managed to buy seventy acres of the Ingliston estate, and in 1960 put on the first show there. At other times of the year the show ground is used for motor racing, though the cars in this picture seem docile enough.

From Edinburgh to Glasgow by rail is a distance of forty-six miles which today takes just a little over forty minutes, whereas the first train between the two cities, set in motion by the Edinburgh and Glasgow Railway Company, took two and a quarter hours. That was in 1842. Six years later the North British Railway station was completed and called Waverley Station (one more indication of the power exerted by the works of Sir Walter Scott). Below the Castle Rock, in the bottom left of the picture, there used to be a loch, which was drained in the eighteenth century as plans for the creation of the New Town were being hatched over on the north side of what is now Princes Street, and the channel it left behind made a perfect passage for the railway track. Meanwhile, the old town went out of fashion. Parts of it are still there, however. The winding ribbon of road on the right is Johnston Terrace which at its apex meets the Royal Mile, about to start its journey downhill from the Castle to Holyrood. Compared to other British cities, the capital of Scotland has evaded the tastelessness of most modern architects, but there have been a few mishaps, such as the appalling Saint James Centre, in the top left of the picture. It may confidently be supposed that Saint James would have deplored it.

△ Edinburgh, Midlothian, Lothian

'This dream in masonry and living rock', was how Robert Louis Stevenson described Edinburgh in the 1870s. A few bumps have appeared on the townscape since then, but much of what you see here was what he saw too. In the whole of the United Kingdom there is no city quite so stimulating to the eye as Edinburgh. Its most famous, and most magnificent, feature projects conspicuously in the foreground of this photograph: a blending of the skills of man with the accidents of nature. Edinburgh Castle's oldest building, St Margaret's Chapel of 1076, is the oldest in the entire city; and additions have been made to the castle ever since. Another place of interest stands on a square of open ground just behind: George Heriot's Hospital was begun in 1628, out of funds bequeathed by Jinglin' Geordie, the king's treasurer. But the strangest sight in Edinburgh is undoubtedly Arthur's Seat, virtually a mountain in the middle of the city, rising out of Holyrood Park, with, on its west side, the basaltic comb of rock called Salisbury Crags.

▽ Holyrood, Edinburgh

First-time visitors to Edinburgh usually have in mind at least two essential sights: the castle and the palace. Holyrood – comprising the abbey, the park and the palace – begins at the northern slope of Arthur's Seat. The original palace was begun in about 1500 by James IV, but was burnt down during English invasions in the 1540s. It was rebuilt but then destroyed again during one of Cromwell's expeditions. Once more it was rebuilt; so the structure we see today is substantially different from the original Palace of Holyroodhouse, and quite different also from that in which Mary Queen of Scots spent six tragic years – tragedy which in the course of time has come to seem like romance. When the present Queen is in town a flag flies from the front (not on this day, however) and the Duke of Edinburgh is often among the early morning strollers in the park behind.

New Town, Edinburgh ▷

In 1767 it was announced in Edinburgh that the architect James Craig was to be 'entitled to the primum for the best plan of a New Town'. This plan became the streets and squares which are today bounded by St Andrews Square to the east, Charlotte to the west, and Queen and Princes Street to the north and south. A dozen or more developments followed, utilizing the talents of such architects as Robert Adam and William Playfair, and the results of these are today known collectively as the New Town. Their only unifying feature, apart from the classical symmetry of their architecture, is the sandstone from Craigleith quarry of which the houses were constructed. This segment was among the last to be completed. It was built in the 1830s and includes (from left to right) Douglas, Eglinton, Glencairn and Grosvenor Crescents – each joined to Palmerston Place – and Melville Street running east from St Mary's Cathedral (not added for another half century or so). Cleaning operations frequently restore the grey buildings of a certain block or street to the original honey-coloured hue but such is the stone's absorbency that before long it is blackening again. Never mind – some residents prefer their classicism in sombre grey.

▽ **Linlithgow**, West Lothian, Lothian

One of Scotland's oldest royal burghs, Linlithgow was a common stopover for important personages in the Middle Ages. Today the ruins of the fortified Linlithgow Palace are exceptionally well preserved. Its oldest part is the tower in the right foreground, which was built in 1302. The small octagonal tower on the left, called Queen Margaret's Bower, is where the Queen awaited news of her husband James IV's encounter with the English at Flodden, only to learn of his death. In front of the palace is the church of Saint Michael, generally called the cathedral. Consecrated sixty years before the foundation of the palace, it was destroyed by fire in 1424 and has been much rebuilt and restored since – the latest addition being Geoffrey Clarke's spiky crown, put into place by helicopter in 1964. Before it, the High Street, old style and new, branches to the east and the west; and behind is the small loch, still popular with local sailors, and the M9 motorway, stretching to Stirling, Perth, and eventually Wick.

◁ **Leith**, Midlothian, Lothian

Until this century one of the regular means of approaching Scotland from London and further afield was by sea. It was popular, too, the fare being roughly half of what it cost to travel by rail (although the journey from London took thirty hours). Once the east of Scotland's busiest port, Leith has a rather forlorn atmosphere in this age of the plane and the articulated lorry. But it is still used by cargo ships and at night Leith's streets and pubs do their best to contain the exuberance of their crews. To refer to Leith as a part of Edinburgh is a mistake not to be made in the presence of an inhabitant of either: the port was a separate municipality until 1920 and remains proud of its independence. Here we are given some impression of the harbour's complexity; happily a few ships appear to be in business. If it's facts and figures you want, then, as so often, William McGonagall supplies them all:

> And as for the Docks, they are magnificent to see,
> They comprise five docks, two piers, 1,141 yards long respectively.

Pladda, Bute, Strathclyde

This lonely teardrop in the Firth of Clyde is one of seven islands comprising the county of Bute. It is not quite as remote as our photograph might suggest, however – Pladda is swimming distance from Kildonan, on the southern tip of the Island of Arran, across the Sound of Pladda. The raised land on which the lighthouse was built in 1826 suggests that it was once even smaller. Hulking in the distance – deceptively close – is Ailsa Craig.

Inchcolm, Fifeshire, Fife ▷

The oddly shaped 'inch' is surely the strangest of the Firth of Forth islands. Its abbey (the Abbey of the Inch of Saint Columba) was founded in the twelfth century by Alexander I, out of gratitude to a hermit who had offered him shelter during a stormy passage on the Forth. It consists of a thirteenth-century church, an octagonal chapter house and a cloister. The abbey ceased to function after the Reformation and later became a burial place for the Morays. It is composed mainly of greenstone, with bands of mica and sandstone and much fertile soil besides. The island was much abused by the English, but one Englishman gave it a place in literature: in *Macbeth*, the Thane of Ross, reporting Macbeth's victory over the Norsemen, informs Duncan: 'Sweno, the Norways' King, craves composition; nor would we deign him burial of his men, till he disbursed at St Colme's inch ten thousand dollars to our general use.'

◁ Forth Road and Rail Bridges,
West Lothian, Lothian and Fifeshire, Fife

A bridge over to Fife from Edinburgh was long called for, but the shortest distance from the capital itself across the Firth of Forth is five miles. So the points chosen were South Queensferry, eight miles from Edinburgh, and North Queensferry across the water. The Forth Bridge, designed by Benjamin Baker and John Fowler, opened for traffic on 4 March 1890. Including the approach viaducts, its total length is one mile, 1005 yards. It cost over three million pounds and took seven years to build — but the painting of it is a famously never-ending task. The network of steel tubes knitted together by lattice-work is still an awesome sight, more so than the road bridge — though it makes a good contrast — which opened in 1964.

River Forth, Stirlingshire, Central ▷

A crook o' the Forth
Is worth an earldom o' the north.

The old rhyme bears witness to the quality of this alluvial land, watered by the River Forth between Stirling, just below, and the Firth of Forth. As we fly with the crow, it is just over five miles from Stirling to Alloa, the little manufacturing and brewing town on the north bank in the middle distance, but the Links o' the Forth, as this stretch is called, measures more than twelve miles. The wells of the Forth are miles away from here again, 3000 feet up on the north side of Ben Lomond. This picture shows that all the words we use to describe rivers — 'snaky', 'serpentine', 'meandering', and so on — are fully justified by geography.

◁ **Stirling Castle,** Stirlingshire, Central

Stirling Castle, and the town itself, played an important role in the thirteenth- and fourteenth-century Wars of Independence; near here Bannockburn was fought and, seventeen years earlier, William Wallace routed the Earl of Surrey's army at Stirling Bridge. The castle, still under military occupation, has been much destroyed, rebuilt and refashioned, and the present buildings date mainly from the Renaissance. On its 250-foot basaltic rock, Stirling Castle bears a resemblance to that of Edinburgh, both from the ground and from the air.

Dunfermline, Fifeshire, Fife ▷

Words in stone network round the crown of the abbey tower read 'King Robert the Bruce'. Here, before the high altar, the great hero of the medieval Wars of Independence is buried. Dunfermline's Benedictine abbey dates from the twelfth century, but lettering such as that on the east portion could only have been carried out by the crudest of Victorian gothic revivalists. Enough of the church remains, however, to make it an important ecclesiastical monument. The groundwork and wall of the adjoining monastic buildings stimulate the imagination to thoughts of a Scottish monk's day-to-day business in the Middle Ages. That very Victorian millionaire who bestowed over 2500 libraries on the world, Andrew Carnegie, was born in 1835 in Moody Street, Dunfermline, in a small cottage which is still standing, as is the first of his generous gifts, in Abbot Street.

Loch Leven, Kinross-shire, Tayside

Castle Island is not the largest on Loch Leven (St Serf's is) but it is certainly the most famous, a distinction arising out of the island's connection with Mary Queen of Scots. During the years 1567–8, she was imprisoned here, the unwilling guest of Lady Douglas, and was forced to abdicate in favour of her son, leaving her half-brother, Moray, as regent. Willie Douglas, a youth of eighteen, smuggled the Queen out of the castle while the residents were at prayer and rowed her ashore, dropping the keys of the castle in the loch. (They were recovered 300 years later.) Poor Mary could not avoid misfortune, however: two weeks later her army was defeated at Langside (now part of Glasgow) and she fled to England where she was imprisoned again and eventually executed. Loch Leven, I almost forgot to say, is also famous for its trout fishing. The town of Kinross nestles in the background.

Gleneagles and Blackford,
Perthshire, Tayside

Though the first association with 'Gleneagles' (*above*) is likely to be the golf courses and hotel, there is in fact a glen of that name running through the Ochil Hills a little to the south. Moreover, the name has nothing to do with birds, deriving from the Gaelic *eaglais*, a church. The main courses, the King's and Queen's, were laid out in 1918 with the help of the famous golfer, James Braid; the hotel opened five years later and two more courses have been added since. If not the hardest in the country to play, they are certainly the most beautiful.

Two miles away in the Strathallan Valley (*left*) is the village of Blackford, in the same parish as the golf hotel. Here we look southwards on the village and its chequerboard surrounds, and, cupped in the Ochils, the Upper Glen Devon Reservoir. Brewing was once a strong industry here, but the Scottish brewers have fared worse than their English counterparts under the thumb of big business, and consequently real Scotch ale is taking longer to return to its proper place alongside whisky as part of the Scot's staple diet.

41

Dysart, Fifeshire, Fife ▷

In Walter Scott's novel *Rob Roy*, Andrew Fairservice, the loquacious gardener, refers to the kingdom of Fife as 'just like a great combined city – Sae mony royal boroughs yoken on end to end ... Kirkcaldy, the sell o't, is langer than ony town in England.' He was mostly right, and indeed there was a touch of prophecy in it: Kirkcaldy, though hardly by itself longer than any English town, is still called 'the lang toun'. It ate up the once independent burgh of Dysart in 1930. As with much of the surrounding area, the main industry of this town which faces Edinburgh across the Firth of Forth is coalmining, with records for the earliest mines going back to 1424. Black stone apart, the men of Dysart once made nails: twelve million of them a year, roughly, at the turn of the eighteenth and nineteenth centuries. This picture gives a fine view of the welcoming arms of the harbour.

◁ **Alva, Clackmannanshire, Central**

Built on the last squares of the alluvial plain which spreads from the River Forth at Alloa, south of here, to the start of the Ochil Hills, splendidly apparent before us, Alva is a compact hillfoot town in the Devon Valley. Alva Burn feeds the Devon River, meandering by at the foot of our picture, upon which was built the town's textiles industry, now making knitwear and tartan shawls. During the eighteenth century silver was mined in the hills to the rear (hence Silver Glen, leading down to the town), the highest of which, Ben Cleuch, is at the extreme right. The Devon River has its source just there too, but in order to reach the point at which it is visible here, it takes a very long way round, making a U-turn several miles to the east.

Castle Campbell,
Clackmannanshire, Central

When it came into the hands of the Earl of Argyll through marriage in the fifteenth century, this castle was known as Castle Gloom. The hill beside is still Gloomhill, and the burns which run down on either side are the Burn of Sorrow and the Burn of Care (sometimes known together as the waters of grief); what is more, the whole lot is situated in the parish of Dollar ('dolour'). The Earl need not have been a superstitious man, then, to change its name to Castle Campbell. The switch did him little good: the place was besieged several times in the succeeding century and finally burned by the greatest vandal of all, Oliver Cromwell, in 1654.

44

Transworld Oil Rig, North Sea
Supply Ship, Leith, Midlothian, Lothian ▷

The seventies in Scotland were the decade of black gold – or so it seemed at the time, as vested interest groups slugged it out in the press, and on TV and in speeches to see who could gain most political advantage from drilling for oil. Some even believed (or said they did) that a reincarnated Scotland – one with its own political, decision-making apparatus, like other nations – could be nourished on the stuff. Well, we are ten years older, a little wiser (perhaps), and divested of illusions now. It has long been evident that the only parts of Scotland to benefit from drilling and digging are those, such as Aberdeen, where the industry is actually based.

An oil rig or derrick (which this is) is the steel structure from which wells are drilled, whereas an oil platform (for which the rig is often mistaken) is the steel or concrete construction placed over the ground where the oil has been found. The cost of building a rig in 1974 (roughly when this one was constructed) was about $25,000 a day. Even with current technology, however, it is possible to recover only half of the oil reserves in the ground.

Work on the rigs and platforms goes on round the clock. This one at Leven may or may not have been serviced by this ship docked at Leith.

◁ **Crail**, Fifeshire, Fife

The coast road north from Edinburgh to Saint Andrews and Tayside is for part of its route a series of links between small medieval fishing villages of similar appearance: St Monance, Pittenweem, Anstruther and, the most north-easterly, Crail. James VI called these royal burghs the fringe of gold on a grey cloth mantle. Because of its position, Crail was once the base of smugglers. But times change and now its pretty white houses are occupied by artists. Many are owned and restored by the National Trust for Scotland. The fishing industry flourished here in the eighteenth and nineteenth centuries (to which it owes its present healthy appearance) but fishermen everywhere in Scotland today are unhappy and pessimistic, and in many places are seeking other types of catch, such as shellfish. Crail has a reputation for lobsters, and boats for this and more conventional kinds of fishing are in and out of its harbour still.

Anstruther, Fifeshire, Fife ▷

Anstruther, for those who like this kind of thing, should properly be known as the 'United Burgh of Kilrenny, Cellardyke, Anstruther Easter and Anstruther Wester', which has a certain fascination but not enough to make it memorable to the hundreds of children who come here on their annual summer holidays. You can still buy your fish in the morning just as the catch is being landed at Anstruther harbour, but the town no longer holds its place as the centre of Scotland's herring fishing. There are a few boats in the harbour now but no holiday-makers, for this is autumn and the east coast has a way of inviting cold. The road dividing the browning fields behind is the direct route north to St Andrews; it takes you longer by the Crail road (where R.L. Stevenson once stayed while training to be an engineer) but it's worth it.

St Andrews Cathedral and Castle, Fifeshire, Fife

The importance of St Andrews in medieval Scottish history can be gauged from the rise and fall of its cathedral, the oldest in Scotland: it was begun in 1161 by Bishop Arnold, consecrated in the presence of Robert the Bruce in 1318, and effectively finished off by John Knox in 1559; that is, it was violated after his sermon on the 'Cleansing of the Temple'. The process of dereliction continued for many years afterwards, as the townspeople carried off the stones and used them for different purposes, mostly secular. All that remains now are parts of the south nave and transept walls, the east and west doorway, and St Regulus' square tower, which predates the cathedral itself and is the oldest building in the city (*c.* 1100). West of the cathedral, along the shore to our left, are the fringes of the Royal and Ancient Golf Club – if no longer the ecclesiastical capital of Scotland, St Andrews can justly claim to be the golfing capital of the world – which consists of four courses. In keeping with the democratic traditions of Scotland, they belong to the Links Trust and on payment of a fee are open to anyone, without the need of an introduction.

Between the cathedral and the golf course stand the ruins of the thirteenth-century castle (*left*), much in use during the Scottish Reformation. It fell into neglect in the seventeenth century, but still has its bottle dungeon where Reformers were held and, after them, their persecutor Cardinal Beaton – dead, salted and awaiting 'what exsequies the bishops would prepare for him', as Knox gloatingly concluded.

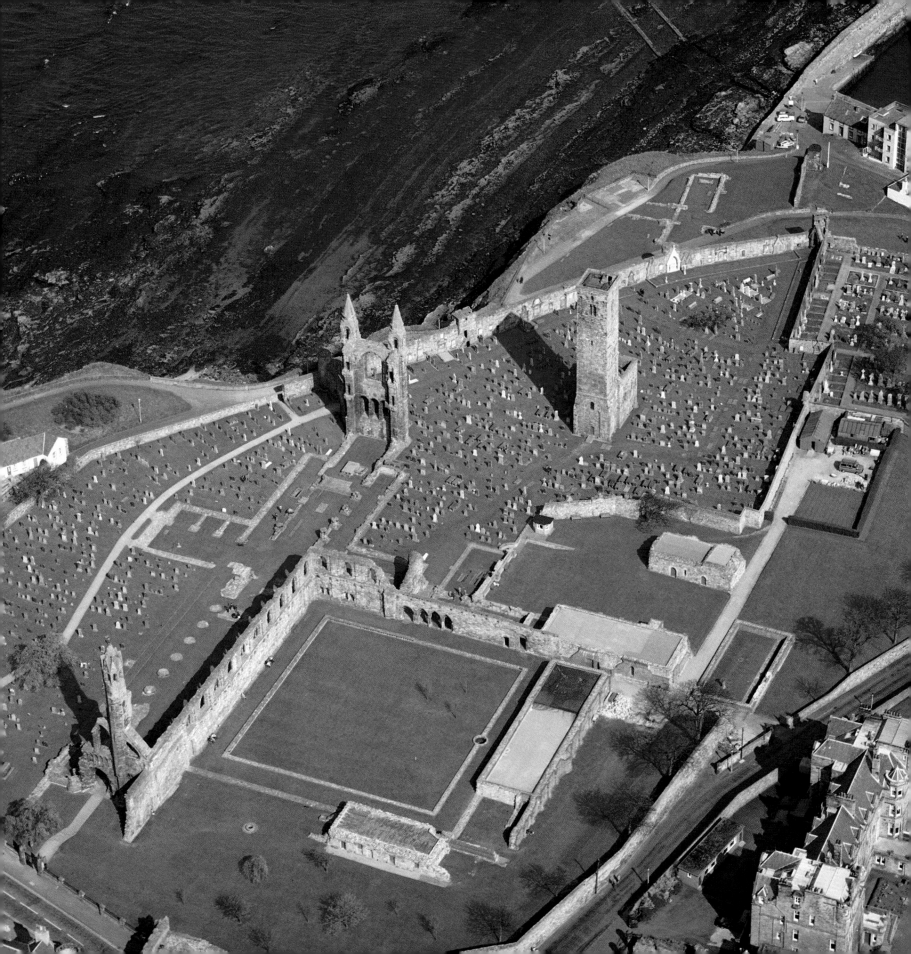

Perth, Perthshire, Tayside

Until the mid-fifteenth century St John's Town (the old name for Perth survives in the local football team) was the principal seat of the kingdom of Scotland. However, reforming zeal in the late Middle Ages not only diminished its official status but also destroyed most of its important sites, which means that small evidence of its national importance is visible today. Far less of its Roman origins. Modern Perth, however, has a healthy complexion and is noted for whisky blending, weaving and, not least, dry cleaning. Our picture, looking north over the Queen's and Perth bridges, gives a clear impression of how it still manages to offer its 40,000 inhabitants the advantages of both town and country life.

◁ **Blair Atholl,** Perthshire, Tayside

△ **Loch Faskally,** Perthshire, Tayside

Since its foundation in 1269, Blair Castle, seat of the Duke of Atholl (still the largest landowner in Perthshire) has been dismantled and rebuilt more than once. After bombardment during the campaign that led up to Culloden in 1746, the castle was renovated in keeping with contemporary fashion – all turrets and parapets removed. But when the nineteenth-century occupants decided it was time to do it up again, their rebuilding was in keeping with the Victorian fancy for Scotch baronial – so all the turrets and parapets were put back on again. Glen Garry, along which we look here, is refreshed by the River Tilt as it dashes down to meet the Garry. Its present greenery can in a small way be attributed to Robert Burns who, on visiting the Falls of Bruar nearby and finding the spot treeless, wrote 'The Humble Petition of Bruar Water':

Would, then, my noble master please
  To grant my highest wishes,
He'll shade my banks wi' tow'ring trees
  And bonie spreading bushes.

The Duke obliged, of course.

The River Tummel runs in and out of the narrow strip of the loch of the same name before uniting with the River Garry just south of the Pass of Killiecrankie. Until 1950 the river then continued its flow through the town of Pitlochry to join the Tay, but in that year a dam was constructed just north of the town as part of the North of Scotland Hydro-Electric Board's Tummel Valley scheme. So the two-and-a-half-mile-long Loch Faskally was created, enhancing what was already one of Scotland's most celebrated beauty spots. The Pass of Killiecrankie, just to the north through the glens, is where Viscount Dundee fought and won a battle for the Jacobite cause in 1689; the victory was ultimately futile, however, and he lost his own life into the bargain.

Carn Mor Dearg,
Inverness-shire, Highland

In Scotland, hundreds of thousands of names —
of towns, villages, rivers, glens, mountains and
islands — are in Gaelic, names first spoken in
what until 150 years ago was the native language of large parts of the country. (There are
80,000 Gaelic speakers in Scotland today.) Carn
Mor Dearg roughly translated means 'great red
stone'. A few hundred feet smaller than the
thoroughly anglicized Ben Nevis at 4012 feet, it
is connected to the latter mountain by an *arête*,
or ridge. Hardy walkers can pass, if they wish,
from one mountain to another by way of this
ridge; they will find the glen between Ben Nevis
and the great red granite mountain green and
welcoming, especially after experiencing the
snow that lingers higher up during most of the
year.

Loch Avon, Banffshire, Grampian ▷

The Cairngorms are not the preserve of skilled
and well-equipped mountaineers; apart from
the ski routes with their merciful chairlifts, they
contain many paths for the adventurous walker.
To reach Loch Avon, a narrow trench of water
bulldozed into shape by an Ice Age glacier
between Cairn Gorm (4084 feet) and Ben Macdui
(4296), you have to be prepared to trudge all the
way up Glen Derry, skirting the flanks of some
of Britain's highest mountains (six of the Cairn-
gorm peaks are above 4000 feet). Here we look
south-west at Ben Macdui's ankles, and the
stream trickling into the loch from its source a
mile or so away. Passing by in 1861, Queen
Victoria could not help noticing that 'the snow
. . . has such fine effect.'

Dundee Law and Tay Bridges,
Angus, Tayside

Some would say that while the showpieces of Edinburgh and Aberdeen are Scotland's pretty face, the industrial cities, Glasgow and Dundee, are its soul. Whether you accept that formula or not, there is no sense in pretending that the codewords for industrial Dundee – 'jute, jam and journalism' – are as readily applicable now as they once were. The eastern port's prominence in the world's jute industry lasted roughly from the middle of the last century to the middle of the present one, allowing for some dips in between. Today, most of the great factories are closed or have been converted to other uses (the

largest of them, Baxter's mills in Princes Street, covered an area of nine acres). The invention of marmalade took place in Dundee when a merchant unexpectedly found himself in possession of a quantity of Seville oranges, which his ingenious wife transformed into something later called Keiller's Marmalade. (The firm is still in business.) Journalism is still here, under the banner of the firm of D.C. Thomson, which publishes an assortment of weekly magazines and comics, plus the *Sunday Post* newspaper.

To the traveller entering Dundee by either of the Tay Bridges (*overleaf*), the 571-foot volcanic

eminence known as the Law (*below*) is the most conspicuous sight. The monument at the peak of its helter-skelter slopes commemorates the dead in the 1914–18 war, and the view from the top encompasses St Andrews, the Grampians and, on the other side of the Firth, the villages of Newport-on-Tay and Tayport. The rail bridge and its predecessor (plus the water which flows under it) are the subject of many poems by one of Dundee's most famous men, the great McGonagall (though he was in fact born in Edinburgh of Irish parents). The best-known of all his poems must be that which marks the disaster of 1879, when ninety passengers on a train were killed when a January gale brought down Sir Thomas Bouch's original rail bridge:

So the train mov'd slowly along the Bridge of
　Tay,
Until it was about midway,
Then the central girders with a crash gave
　way,
And down went the train and passengers into
　the Tay!

▽ Glamis Castle, Angus, Tayside

The association of Glamis with Shakespeare's Macbeth is historically vague; the present structure dates mainly from the last quarter of the seventeenth century, by which time the Englishman who wrote the greatest Scottish play was long dead. However, a building of some sort was on this site before, and a king – Malcolm II, not Duncan – may have been murdered in it or nearby in 1034. There is toil and trouble too in its past, though of a slightly different kind from that suggested by Shakespeare's three witches: Lady Glamis herself was burned for witchcraft in 1537, twenty-seven years before the poet's birth. The present building, all battlements and turrets, was the home of the present Queen and Queen Mother during their childhoods, and Princess Margaret was born at Glamis in 1930. And there is yet another noble connection, in the legend that one of the Earls of Crawford plays forever in a hidden chamber with 'the Devil's buiks', because he sold his soul to Old Nick.

Brechin, Angus, Tayside ▷

A centre for the manufacture of linen and paper, Brechin slopes down to settle on the north bank of the River South Esk in the county of Angus. The town is sometimes blamed for being the place where, in 1296, John Balliol, King of Scots, handed over the realm of Scotland to Edward I of England, whereas in fact that ignoble event took place four miles north of here in Stracathro. The successful Wars of Independence which followed represent a vital symbol in the living Scottish conscience, the Scot's oldest proof that he or she is separate. Brechin Cathedral was founded in 1150. The present building is mainly thirteenth-century, but it suffered a great deal at the hands of the Reformers three centuries later. It was dealt another blow in 1807 – this time in the interests of 'modernization', which destroyed the choir and transepts. Restorers have been at work since then, happily, and have even uncovered some ancient features, such as a fine west window. The building's chief glory, however, is its Celtic tower, of a type rare anywhere outside Ireland. Eighty-seven feet high, it was erected in the tenth century by Irish clergymen, with a door six feet off the ground for defence.

Montrose, Angus, Tayside

The approach to Montrose, which is mainly to the fore of the road and rail bridges, is spectacular and curious, for the town is built on a tongue between the Montrose Basin and the North Sea, and the River South Esk cuts across it, flowing through the two-mile-square basin into the sea. The sandflats in this picture have that sleepy, half-in half-out look permanently. Montrose was once an important Scottish town, figuring largely in the thirteenth-century Wars of Independence, but it has settled for a subsidiary role in the life of the new Scotland: Montrose harbour is now a marine service base for North Sea oil exploration.

Curious also, for a town of this size, are its literary associations: Lewis Grassic Gibbon was born and raised nearby and Hugh MacDiarmid, Scotland's greatest twentieth-century literary genius, lived and worked here (as editor of the *Montrose Review*) and here consolidated his friendship with another poet, Edwin Muir, who once rescued him from a lavatory.

Arbroath, Angus, Tayside ▷

Samuel Johnson passed by here on his tour of Scotland in 1773 and, amid never-ending complaints about the absence of trees, applauded the 'venerable edifice' of Arbroath's red sandstone abbey, concluding, 'I should scarcely have regretted my journey had it afforded nothing more than the sight of Aberbrothick.' Aberbrothick (or '-ock'), as Arbroath was then called, derives its name from the Brothock water which flows into the harbour we look down on here. In the popular mind it may be associated mainly with kippers and the highest score ever recorded in senior football – 36–0, against Bon Accord in 1885 – but the town ought to inspire first the memory of the Declaration of Arbroath, which was signed here to proclaim the independence of Scotland in 1320, after Bruce had liberated the nation from English armies.

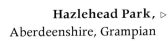 **Dunnottar Castle,**
Kincardineshire, Grampian

The sea is not always this calm and together with the cliffs, roughly 200 feet high, and the deep chasm on the landward side, it makes plain why Dunnottar Castle, two miles south of Stonehaven on the east coast, was for centuries a favourite stronghold of the power-hungry Scottish nobility (and, on occasion, of the even hungrier English). Romantic? Life here in the Middle Ages would have been less luxurious than in the average contemporary prefab, and the stone floors were frequently stained with blood. Dunnottar was the stage for many conflicts until the 1715 rebellion, after which it began to deteriorate. Some years before that, 167 Covenanters – members of a Presbyterian resistance – were held in the Whigs' Vault, a barbarous dungeon open to the sea. During a mass breakout, about ten of them escaped and the rest were killed or recaptured and punished. Times change; it's now a museum.

Hazlehead Park, ▷
Aberdeenshire, Grampian

Mazes became popular in British gardens in the Elizabethan period, at about the same time as fountains, topiary and statues. Before being formalized, however, circular mazes (or 'mismazes') were common on village greens for use in games or celebrations. The precise derivation is obscure, but Roman children in Britain no doubt 'trod the maze' and the game may even be related to the Cretan labyrinth, or be a symbol of the winding life which eventually leads to Jerusalem, the name given to the centre of the maze. This one, of privet, is in a park three miles west of Aberdeen. It was planted in 1935. The park itself has been common ground since the fourteenth century, originating in the Freedom Lands which were granted to the city by Robert the Bruce.

67

◁ Braemar, Aberdeenshire, Grampian

It was in Braemar that the Royal Standard was raised in 1715, to which call 12,000 men rallied in support of the Jacobite cause and the Old Pretender. (The exact spot of the raising of the standard is now covered by a hotel.) Given the ultimate failure of that expedition, there is irony in the fact that the town on the Clunie Water is nowadays best known for being the site of the annual Royal Highland Gathering, which the present royal family eagerly attend from their place down the road at Balmoral. Here we catch the River Dee near its Highland source, running from the mountains in the background eastwards to the North Sea, as straight and purposefully as rivers can run. The Clunie Water tumbles down from Glen Clunie, dividing the town in the shadow of the Morrone Hill, joining the Dee to help it on its way through the valley to Aberdeen.

Banchory, Kincardineshire, Grampian ▷

Seventeen miles south-west of Aberdeen, with a population of just over 2000, Banchory sits comfortably on the River Dee, a pleasant stopping place for those following the river back into its Highland beginnings. Indeed, hills in the distance and hidden from sight on the right bank of the river foretell the shape of the landscape just fifteen or so miles further on in the direction of Braemar. The town is favoured by salmon-fanciers, too – some of whom intend to hook them, others simply to admire the leap where the Water of Feugh meets the Dee, not far behind us.

69

Aberdeen, Aberdeenshire, Grampian ▷

The name signifies the confluence of the River Don and the River Dee, the two arteries upon which the great north-eastern city has developed and prospered. Before the last war, Aberdeen's main industries were shipbuilding and fishing, but now it is the northern capital of the European oil industry. Although the business this has brought is imposed from without rather than developed from within (the multi-national companies have their offices here because this is where the action is — when it ceases to be so they will leave) the activity has given present-day Aberdeen a healthy appearance. Perhaps its real fame rests on stone, however, the hard, uncompromising grey Rubislaw granite. This material distinguishes it from other cities not only in Scotland but the world, a fact which strikes the visitor on his first walk along Union Street — that dead straight line in the middle of the picture. Union Street's mile was laid out in 1800; it is composed mainly of three-storey fronts, stopping at the eastern end in the baronial Salvation Army Citadel. Here we look at the back of that building, down to the fork of Holborn Street and Albyn Place. Old Aberdeen — a separate municipality until the nineteenth century — is behind us.

Docks, Aberdeen ▷

The centre of the Aberdeen fish market is here, on the Albert Basin by the River Dee. By the hour at which this picture was taken the trawler fleet has landed, auctioned its catch and dispersed in search of light relief before another early start next morning. The fishing boats appear to be keeping themselves to themselves over on the Albert Quay, while some oil-related business is going on nearer to us on the Torry Harbour.

◁ Peterhead, Aberdeenshire, Grampian

The immediate association with Peterhead in most people's minds used to be fishing. During the nineteenth century the town was a centre for British whaling, which then gave way to herring fishing, which in turn was replaced by white fish. Since the mid-seventies, however, the first word to follow Peterhead as well as Aberdeen has been 'oil'. Peterhead's most famous feature is still its huge harbour, of which we see in this picture only the north arm and the tip of the long southern breakwater. The pink granite town is nowadays used as a North Sea oil service and supply base. This makes it difficult to imagine its fame at the end of the eighteenth century as a fashionable spa, when warm baths were constructed for the pleasure of an upper-class clientele.

Fraserburgh, Aberdeenshire, Grampian ▷

In the nineteenth century new towns and villages founded by landowners on the east coast of Scotland prospered because of their fishing industries. Fraserburgh's complex harbour, covering twenty-seven acres with two and a half miles of landing space, made it one of the major fishing towns in the Aberdeenshire area, and although oil is the latest word for prosperity, there are fishing boats in the harbour still. Built on Kinnaird Head, the north-eastern point at which Scotland's coastline turns the corner and runs along to Banff and Inverness, Sir Alexander Fraser's sixteenth-century burgh now has a population of 11,000. One curious, and oft-forgotten, feature of the place is that for ten years (between 1595–1605) Fraserburgh was a university town. However, the first principal fell foul of the king, got himself arrested, and the institution foundered.

△ **Portknockie Golf Course,**
Banffshire, Grampian

Craigellachie △
Banffshire, Grampian

Duffus Castle, ▷
Morayshire, Grampian

The sands of Cullen Bay are pitted with lost golf balls, for this eighteen-hole course is laid out on the raised bench between Cullen and Portknockie. The passage of glaciers in Scotland during the Ice Age contributed greatly to the present appearance of the landscape: not only do the valleys take their U-shape from the weight of the glaciers, but when the ice finally melted the release resulted in raised land like this over much of the coast.

Craigellachie stands on the River Spey a mile or less from Charlestown of Aberlour, and is among the most famous haunts of Scotland's surrogate patron saint, John Barleycorn. Warlike spirits are indeed contained in bottles hereabouts: 'Stand fast!', slogan (or battle cry) of the local Clan Grant, was snatched during the last century and domesticated as the name of one of this region's best-known products.

The early Scottish castles, Norman in design, consisted of a mound called a 'motte', which was basically earth turned out of the moat (itself an essential feature) on which was erected a timber keep annexed in an enclosure called a bailey. The mound and ditch of Duffus are what remain of the castle in which David I stayed in 1151; the remainder was put up 200 years later. The tower, built on a mound not designed to support it, has split. Much else has changed since the fourteenth century, for the waters of Loch Spynie once lapped against the castle surrounds. After several failed attempts over many years, the loch was drained in the early nineteenth century, and survives only as a largish pond five miles away.

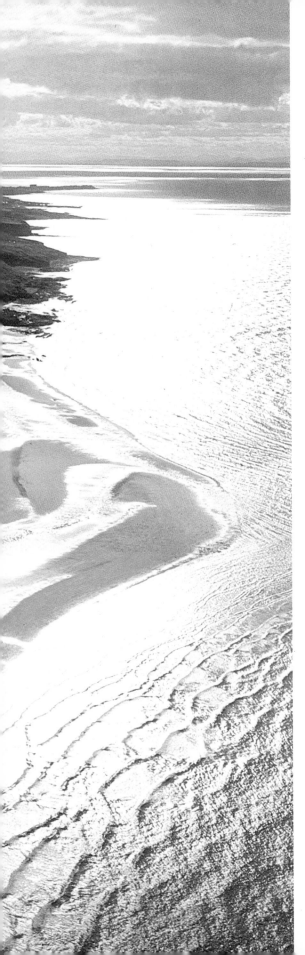

Covesea Skerries Lighthouse,
Morayshire, Grampian

The coast on this stretch of land between Lossiemouth and Hopeman is generally low and flat, with miles of fine sand at the sea-shore. Post-Ice Age glacial release created cliffs of red sandstone between sixty and a hundred feet high. The sea has worked at them for centuries now, making caves and stacks and, from off-shore rocks, a chain of skerries which is reputed to have damaged many ships. One hopes that this lighthouse, built in 1844 and visible eigh-teen miles out, has not been a treacherous beacon in its time. Once a busy village, Covesea is now just a few houses; it is popular with holidaymakers who enjoy exploring the caves along the coast, some of which have legends to illuminate the imagination – such as being a hiding-place for rebels during the Forty-five rebellion – and some of which are just damp, uninviting caves.

◁ Tomatin Distillery, Inverness-shire, Highland

'Wi' usquebae, we'll face the devil.' Burns's line is touchily ambiguous (strange how the expression evolved as Dutch and not Scotch courage). The name whisky derives from *uisge-beatha*, meaning in Gaelic the water of life. When it was first drunk is not clear, but there is a record of King James IV tippling at the turn of the fifteenth and sixteenth centuries. Even before then, though, the stuff was being distilled at Tomatin (pronounced like tomato). One can only guess what its relation was to the modern drink, but connoisseurs of malt pronounce Tomatin's product today to be light and peaty. The present works came into operation in 1909, and today are thoroughly mechanized, yielding roughly one million gallons proof per annum.

Loch Beneveian, Inverness-shire, Highland ▷

The important part played by Loch Beneveian (or Beinn a'Mheadhoin) in the north of Scotland's hydro-electricity scheme has impaired its scenery surprisingly little. But the appearance of Glen Affric, where the loch is situated, has nevertheless altered considerably even in the present century. For one thing, the Forestry Commission which owns the land has planted trees everywhere, including the native but endangered Caledonian pine; for another, the level of Loch Beneveian has been artificially raised by the dam and also by water tunnelled in from Loch Mullardoch, running parallel to it a few miles to the north. Here we look over the dam at the east end on to Beinn a'Mheadhoin, rising to just over 2000 feet, from which the loch takes its name.

◁ **Kessock Bridge,**
Inverness-shire, Highland

△ **Inverness,**
Inverness-shire, Highland

△ **Fort Augustus** and **Loch Ness,**
Inverness-shire, Highland

Before the Kessock Bridge opened, linking Inverness with the Black Isle, motorists heading for Invergordon and the north-east had either to take the long road via Beauly or else queue up for the small ferry. That ferry has not sailed since 1981, however. Everything is now enabled to move more quickly than before; the Highlands are a little less self-contained and the world is a little more the same.

The 'capital of the Highlands', situated at the junction of the Moray and Beauly Firths and at the mouth of the River Ness, cannot wholly be blamed for failing to live up to its fine-sounding nickname. Inverness is a pleasant town of 36,000 inhabitants, but few reminders of its history are in view today. Its harbour still takes commercial traffic, though no longer passenger ships, and crossing the Ness Bridge, farthest away from us, you are still likely to encounter a fisherman dreaming of salmon.

'Kilcummin': whether anyone still refers to the town at the southern end of Loch Ness as that I do not know, but it was so called – after one of St Columba's followers – until a fort was erected here in 1729 and named for William Augustus, Duke of Cumberland. He was better known throughout the Highlands as 'Butcher' because of his tactless methods of 'pacification' after the Jacobite defeat at Culloden, the first of the killing blows which destroyed Highland society over the next seventy-five years. Here we have a view of how the Caledonian Canal and the River Oich cut through the town, and also an impression of the zeal of the Forestry Commission, which in recent years has responded to Samuel Johnson's complaint of 1773 that 'the country is totally denuded of wood'. For some reason there is no sign here of the hoary old Loch Ness Monster, but he could be further up north, in the direction of the splendidly named Drumnadrochit.

Loch Choire, Sutherland, Highland ▷

I have no words for this county, and if I had they would be Gaelic and not English. The first moves to stamp out Gaelic culture – language, dress, music, law, economy – began after the Jacobite defeat at Culloden, and continued until the last of the nineteenth-century Highland Clearances. These involved the shifting of whole populations from settlements throughout the Highlands, so that the land could be grazed by sheep more profitably. Evictions and emigration from this vast wilderness continue today. Loch Choire is parallel to Loch Naver, though slightly smaller, on the southern slope of Ben Klibreck. The peat bog to the right of the stream is still in use, judging by the rows of peats stacked up for fuel. The road on the left may be part of an ancient system of Highland paths which connected settlements here with others up and down Loch Naver. Today these villages exist, where they exist at all, as mere patterns on the ground.

◁ **Golspie,** Sutherland, Highland

The train from Inverness northwards into Sutherland makes a wide loop just south of here, travelling roughly forty miles to cover a distance of fifteen miles as the crow flies. It is at Golspie that the track returns to the coast, to which it sticks until reaching the fishing town of Helmsdale, some way north from here. The Sutherland family's castle, Dunrobin, the core of which was built in the thirteenth century for Robert, 3rd Earl of Sutherland (hence 'Dunrobin', hill of Robert), can be seen at the northernmost extremity of Golspie; and to the west, just behind the town on the summit of Ben Bhraggie, is the statue of the first Duke. Some years ago it was dynamited; although such action must be deemed a little reckless, in these parts his name is still not allowed to pass without a reference to the clearances of poor people from the straths which he oversaw.

◁ **Duncansby Head,** Caithness, Highland   △ **John o' Groats,** Caithness, Highland

The Roman geographer Ptolemy in his first century AD map called it the 'clean-cut cape' and you can quite easily see why: Duncansby Head looks like a piece from a giant jigsaw puzzle. These sandstone cliffs drop more than 200 feet to the sea, and the grass grows all the way to the edge, which gives them their neat appearance. The Head is the north-east tip of the country, at the entrance to the Pentland Firth which separates Scotland from Orkney. To the south of Duncansby lighthouse the cliffs are cleft in great gashes (called 'geos'); one of them, just out of view, is arched by a natural bridge. To the north, beyond the sandy beaches, you may pick out the harbour and houses of John o' Groats.

Not the most northerly mainland part of Great Britain – that distinction belongs to Dunnet Head, a promontory some miles to the west of here. But because of its ferry and its north-easterly situation, John o' Groats (supposedly a corruption of de Groot, the name of a fifteenth-century Dutch ferryman) has become a byword for the top end of the United Kingdom. Land's End is 873 miles away. It must be admitted that many a tourist – motorist and walker – has arrived here only to ask himself why he bothered. But although our picture does not give a helpful impression, the view *from* John o' Groats is splendid. And then there is always the opportunity to board the ferry and cross the Pentland Firth to Orkney. The octagonal tower on the nineteenth-century hotel is said to be a remnant of the octagonal house of the eight inheritors of the de Groot fortune. It was built with a door on each side to avoid squabbling among the eight greedy heirs.

▽ Old Man of Hoy, Orkney

Of the forty-nine islands which constitute Orkney (not 'the Orkneys', or 'the Orkney Islands'), Hoy is the second largest, after the island called Mainland. It is only fourteen miles by six, but even so you will have to walk a good six miles to have a look at the Old Man of Hoy, a 450-foot-high columnar stack of red sandstone, cleft from the rockface by the unending force of seas. The first known climb, in 1966, took three days. It can be seen from the mainland of Scotland, but if you were to get this far on Hoy itself, a walk just a little to the north of here would reward you with a view of Orkney, Shetland and Caithness.

Mainland is the largest island in Orkney and Kirkwall is the county town. Roughly one-third of Mainland's 14,000 population lives in this sea port on the neck of land which divides the island into two unequal parts. St Magnus, the great kirk on the left in the shadow, is one of only two in Scotland to retain its pre-Reformation form in a structurally undamaged state (Glasgow is the other). Norse rule of the seventy islands which make up Orkney began about AD 700, reached a peak 300 years later, and ended in 1468 when the Kind of Denmark pledged the islands to James III. The Scots were not kind rulers at first, however, and even today a native of these islands is an Orkneyman before he is a Scotsman. St Magnus Cathedral was founded in 1137 by Earl Rognvald, the nephew of the saint who, while ruler of Orkney, was murdered by his warmongering rival.

The very names of some of the islands and their characteristic features in Orkney have a kind of poetry. Here we look from the north (Shetland behind us) over Eday, one of the northernmost islands of the group, with Calf of Eday in the foreground. Eday's other attendant holms (an old Norse word for an islet) include Muckle Green Holm, Little Green Holm, Faray, Holm of Faray and Rusk Holm. The strip of water separating Eday from the calf is called Calf Sound, and the rising land which overlooks it, Red Head. Only eight miles long, with a narrow waist bearing an airstrip, Eday is largely uncultivable, much of it being heathery moorland and high hills. Still, 130 people live here. Faray, a slice of which is visible to the right, is only half a mile wide by two miles long; it used to have a population of sixty, but they have all since moved on to Eday or beyond, leaving it to the birds.

◁ **Burray,** South Ronaldsay, Orkney

In both First and Second World Wars, Scapa Flow was a busy naval base, and in both wars its defences were penetrated with serious consequences: in 1917 HMS *Vanguard* was torpedoed, and in 1939 it was the turn of HMS *Royal Oak*; both sinkings resulted in heavy loss of life. After 1918 seventy German ships were ordered to the naval station. All were scuttled by their crews and, in time, their bulk was used to block the entrance to Scapa Flow. After the *Royal Oak* sinking, however, a series of causeways was constructed out of concrete blocks, to link South Ronaldsay to Mainland, and was called the Churchill Barrier. This is one of several which, after completion, left decomposing wrecks like these all over the surrounding beaches. Today Scapa Flow is again busy with marine activity, but this time the cause is oil.

◁ Stornoway, Lewis, Western Isles

The Island of Lewis, like much of the Highlands and Islands, has in recent years found itself in conflict with a monster called 'progress'. In this case, the beast is machine-driven and speaks English. There are two notable examples of the struggle. The first occurred in the 1920s when Lord Leverhulme, the island's proprietor, attempted to extend the fishing industry and ran thuddingly aground on the islanders' preference for their traditional way of life, which includes little fishing. Then, in the 1970s, a proposal to streamline the Harris Tweed weaving industry, involving factories with power-driven looms, was rejected by the weavers, who trusted their hands. Good for them, we may say, but then in the first few years of that decade the number of weavers working on the island dropped by half. Lately it is the oil boom which Stornoway, the capital of Scottish Gaeldom, has had to contend with in its constant struggle to protect the native Gaelic culture.

Ullapool, Ross and Cromarty, Highland ▷

The angular gridiron layout betrays Ullapool's utilitarian origins. It was founded in 1788 by the British Fisheries Society in the hope of exploiting to the full the sea's resources (mainly herring) off the north-west of the country. At a slightly later stage Thomas Telford was involved in the venture, but even so it was not wholly successful, and Ullapool ever since has juggled the twin identities of fishing centre and holiday resort. It is pleasantly situated on the north shore of Loch Broom, close enough to the sea to ensure comfortably sandy beaches in and around the town. In summer, holidaymakers enjoy its mixture of advantages: pretty whitewashed streets leading to dance halls and pubs, but just a few minutes' walk away from rural solitude. The ferry for Stornoway in the Outer Hebrides departs every few hours, and still the occasional fishing boat with African or Russian colours turns up in the harbour.

◁ **Deer,** Highland

Red deer are a commoner sight in the Highlands than you might think. The appearance of a herd on the crest of a hill, or scampering across rocks, causes a strange thrill which bears endless repetition. The world must be getting too small for wildlife, however: deer are resented by foresters whose seedlings they feed on, and wept over by conservationists who see them grow scraggy in winter for lack of nourishment. Both groups agree there are too many, which pleases those who charge money for the privilege of stalking and shooting them. Only one of this herd of stags pauses to size up the noisy enemy above, while his fellows dash blindly for cover.

Meall Mor, Ross and Cromarty, Highland ▷

Three miles north-west of Ullapool, at the mouth of Loch Broom, Meall Mor (literally, great lump) overlooks Isle Martin. Since the late eighteenth century the Highland population has suffered steady depletion, so that areas once busy with crofts now constitute a wilderness. Isle Martin itself, for example, used to have a population of more than thirty people who lived by fishing. Incidentally, the island (named after a saint whose chapel ruins remain) is unusual hereabouts in going under its English name, as almost everything else – rivers, mountains, points and forests – has kept its Gaelic title.

Strathaird Point, Skye, Highland

The most publicized visitor ever to come to the Island of Skye was Samuel Johnson, who in 1773 made an arduous – and courageous – journey north from London. His observations were frequently uncomplimentary – 'Such is the laxity of Highland conversation that the inquirer . . . knows less as he hears more' – but the general wit and wisdom of his commentary is sufficient to forestall lasting resentment. In any case, the Hebrides have their own voice: these lines from 'Johnson in the Highlands' by Iain Crichton Smith (a Lewisman) represent the best possible response to the Englishman's surfeit of reason:

A classical sanity considers Skye.
A huge hard light falls across shifting hills.
This mind, contemptuous of miracles

and beggarly sentiment, illuminates
a healthy moderation. But I hear
like a native dog notes beyond his range

the modulations of a queer music
twisting his huge black body in the pain
that shook him also in raw blazing London.

Strathaird (literally, the heights of the valley) is associated with another eighteenth-century celebrity: Prince Charlie stayed in a cave here on his flight from defeat at Culloden. Also to be seen at Strathaird is the Spar Cave, known for its stalactites.

Invertote, Skye, Highland

In all Scottish place names, the prefix 'inver' signifies the mouth of a river; near here the River Tote opens out into the Sound of Raasay. You won't see it from the road, but all up and down the East Trotternish coast sills of basalt such as this can be found, culminating some miles to the north in the spectacular – and often grotesque – manifestations of the Quiraing rock formations.

Waterfall, Skye ▷

Visitors to Skye are often heard complaining about the amount of rain that falls, forgetting, momentarily, that much of the island's colourful garb is tailored by the climate. Waterfalls are among the most attractive accessories; they appear at their best after a shower of rain, and the look of this one suggests there has been some refreshment recently.

Castle Tioram and Loch Moidart,
Argyll, Highland

Loch Moidart runs into the sea via two channels, north and south, and in the latter a rocky mound projects from a sand spit into the loch, becoming an island at high tide. It supports Castle Tioram, or Tirrim, ('the dry castle') but those who wish to see it and its fairy-landscape setting had better be firm of purpose, for the castle is not easily accessible. Its eight-foot-thick curtain walls were built in the mid-fourteenth century, and it was properly inhabited until at least 1715 when Clanranald, coming out for the Old Pretender, ordered it to be burnt behind him, to prevent it falling into the hands of his enemies should he be killed. Moidart was the spot at which, thirty years later, Bonnie Prince Charlie alighted on the Scottish mainland to pursue his claim to the crown.

◁ **Ardnamurchan,** Argyll, Highland

Rock has kept out soil from this peninsula since the glacial retreat about 12,000 years ago. Its exposed position as mainland Scotland's most westerly headland keeps the population down: at present it stands at about 1500, most of whom live on the southern coast. There are fine shell sands at Sanna Bay, on this side, and on the way there is the chance to explore caves and an ancient fort. But you have to be the adventurous sort to get this far on foot, for not even a footpath goes by the little pool, called Lochan an Dobhrain.

▽ **Mingary Castle,** Argyll, Highland

In this castle, on the southern side of the Ardnamurchan peninsula, James IV stayed in 1495 while on a campaign to subdue the recalcitrant Highland chiefs. Mingary Castle predates the King by over 200 years, however, parts of it having been erected in the thirteenth century. A stone's throw from here is the scattered village of Kilchoan and, beyond that, Ardnamurchan Point, from where there is a fine view of the islands of the Inner Hebrides: Coll and Tiree, Mull, Rum, Eigg and Muck. A curiosity of the Point is that its sundial records the time about half an hour later than GMT.

◁ Industrial Estate,
Loch Eil, Inverness-shire, Highland

The site for the Corpach paper and pulp mill was chosen for its accessibility by rail, road and sea; and also, of course, for the forests nearby. Logs go in one end of the mill and paper comes out the other – not yet stacked up in reams but about to be. The site, which holds Britain's first integrated paper mill, was built between 1963 and 1966 and covers eighty acres. Only soft wood is grown in the Highlands, the other types arriving mainly from Canada; 10,000 trees are felled every day to feed it, and still it cannot compete with the larger Scandinavian mills. Corpach compensates for this by producing specialized papers. Fort William is the nearest town; Ben Nevis stamps its great foot in the background.

Great Glen, ▷
Caledonian Canal, Inverness-shire, Highland

Glenmore or Glen of Albyn or Glen Mor nan Albyn or just the Great Glen; whatever you choose to call it, it is the result of a geological fault 420 million years ago which split the country in two. It contains Lochs Ness, Oich and Lochy, and Thomas Telford's Caledonian Canal which links them. Up to 1,400 men at a time worked on the canal, earning one and sixpence a day, over a period of many years. It first opened in 1822 but proved too shallow. Work dragged on, and it was not ready for business again until 1847. Twenty-two miles of canal created a sixty-mile waterway which, although never much of a success commercially, is still appreciated by amateur sailors. General Wade's road slips by unnoticed here beside the (almost) parallel lines of canal and River Lochy. By Gairlochy, where Loch Lochy meets River Lochy, is Loch Lochy Lock. Try saying that after a dram of Dufftown malt.

Crinan Canal, Argyll, Strathclyde

Cutting through the long tongue on the west coast which comprises Knapdale and Kintyre, the Crinan Canal links the Sound of Jura with Loch Fyne. It enabled ships to reach the Western Isles considerably sooner, and with less threat from the weather, than before: the old sea voyage of 130 miles was reduced to eight, and fishermen were especially grateful. However, even such foresight as its engineer and sponsors possessed was unable to prophesy the coming of steam, which effectively rendered the Crinan Canal obsolete. But today it may take as many as eighty yachts a day in summer. It was designed by John Rennie and built between 1793 and 1801, using stone quarried on the Island of Arran. There are fifteen locks and the canal rises sixty feet above sea level at its highest point, which is just north of where we are, looking south-east to Loch Gilp.

Lochan Shira, Argyll, Strathclyde ▷

Putting the natural world to productive use in the Highlands has been done with the minimum of fuss or interference with the landscape — indeed, in places where there are dams a dramatic element has often been added to it. The North of Scotland Hydro-Electric Board has benefited Argyll greatly in the last thirty years, providing employment for the local population in the building trade, as indigenous crafts have faded. Lochan Shira, north of Loch Fyne, is linked by a glen and river of the same name to Loch Shira. Work on the dam started in 1956, and when completed it made the cost of electricity, relative to steam and diesel methods of production, considerably cheaper.

Glencoe, Argyll, Highland

The famous massacre of the 'glen of weeping' was carried out by a gang of 128 soldiers led by Campbell of Glenlyon; his victims were the Macdonalds of Glencoe, whose chief had delayed signing the oath of allegiance, required of all Highland chiefs, to William and Mary, in place of the Stuart James VII. In the notorious events which began at dawn on 13 February 1692, some forty of the 200 inhabitants of the glen were slain. The massacre was in addition a crime against Highland hospitality – the Campbell brigade had lodged with the Macdonalds the night before and participated in a feast – and against the House of Stuart. We Campbells, who have had to live with it ever since, can take some consolation from the fact that although the leading villain was a Campbell, not all his sly killers were necessarily so called. And as great a crime was committed by Sir John Dalrymple, Master of Stair in Edinburgh, who had suppressed Macdonald's papers when they eventually arrived, intending to make an example of him. No one holds it against the Dalrymples.

The small island in Loch Leven (not to be confused with that of the same name in Kinross-shire) is Eilean Munde, where many Macdonalds are buried. Through the glen, on the road beyond which rises to 1011 feet over a distance of twelve miles, there is a pub with a sign which says, 'No Campbells allowed'. Incognito, I've enjoyed many a pint of beer there.

Ben Nevis, Inverness-shire, Highland

The annoying thing about Ben Nevis is that while it is the highest mountain in the United Kingdom (4406 feet) it lacks a definite summit. From Fort William, huddling below on the crook of Loch Eil and Loch Linnhe, which ought to offer the best view, it appears as a rather undistinguished lump. Still, it occupies a special place in the affections of all who have seen it, and especially those who have climbed it. At this close range, its north side looks like an iced chocolate cake which someone has made a rude start on. This face is the preserve of experienced mountaineers, but elsewhere Ben Nevis is easily climbed. On a hot day in summer you will find the great granite mountain surprisingly crowded. Halfway up you may pass an inn, which used to provide refreshment for thirsty walkers, though sadly no longer.

◁ **Ben Cruachan,** Argyll, Strathclyde   △ **Loch Awe,** Argyll, Strathclyde

The twin peaks of Ben Cruachan (pronounced with a stress on the first syllable) are not only better sculpted than anything on Ben Nevis, they are probably more often seen (though not always identified) by travellers in Scotland. Ben Nevis is higher, of course, and so gets all the publicity. The 3695-foot Cruachan can be reached in about four hours from Loch Awe hotel, and if you still feel like walking after that, another four hours in this direction and you could be near Oban. Translated from the Gaelic, Cruachan means 'haunch of peaks'. It was the war cry (or *sluagh-ghairm*, 'slogan') of the Campbells who ruled this region.

'It's a far cry to Loch Awe!' The exact meaning of the old shout is in dispute, but it was probably a confident boast of the inaccessibility of Campbell territory, which includes this twenty-three-mile-long loch. Loch Awe is studded with ancient timber dwellings, called crannogs, and with churches and castles. The castle of the Campbells of Lochawe still stands on an island to the south of here, Innis Chonnel. The ruins in this picture, Kilchurn Castle, are among the more elaborate in the district. The castle was founded by the Breadalbanes in the fifteenth century and stands on a small tongue at the north-east end, where the River Orchy flows through the Strath of Orchy into the loch. It was abandoned in the eighteenth century, and one of its towers was toppled in 1879 by the same gale which brought down the Tay Bridge. The original outflow of Loch Awe was at its southern tip, towards Jura, but the last Ice Age changed all that when glacial moraine became fertile land. Now the loch discharges in the same direction as the road, through the Pass of Brander, into Loch Etive and the Atlantic Ocean.

△ **Eriska** and **Loch Creran,**
Argyll, Strathclyde

Loch Fyne, Argyll, Strathclyde ▷

The entrance to Loch Creran, which makes a passage between the hills of Benderloch to the south and Appin to the north, is shielded by the islet of Eriska, accessible by the small bridge at the bottom right of the picture. For most of its length a road winds round the loch, and at one time a railway track did too, the trains crossing the water at Dallachulish, and then chugging south towards Oban. With the protected waters of Creran on one side and the Barcaldine Forest on the other, it was a pleasant journey. The loch's north shore is the site of the infamous 'Appin Murder' of 1752, in which Colin Campbell, government factor for Appin, who was persecuting the local Stewarts, was shot. The prime suspect, Alan Breck Stewart, disappeared, and James Stewart was tried by a Campbell-heavy jury and hanged. Robert Louis Stevenson used the events, after a bit of typical spit and polish, in *Kidnapped*.

From the head of Loch Fyne, a forty-one-mile-long sea loch, we look along its narrow sleeve, past the inlet of Loch Shira (not to be confused with the lochan – or small loch – of the same name at the opposite end of the glen) to Furnace and eventually Knapdale. The road running in from the left of our picture is from Arrochar; you won't see them here, but at the foot of the next glen, called Hell's Glen, are some white stones which mark the traditional place of betrothal for the Argyll tinkers.

◁ Oban harbour and McCaig's Folly

The circular tower bearing a superficial resemblance to the Colosseum in Rome is conspicuous everywhere you go in Oban, but even a close inspection is unlikely to bring many clues about its origins. Is this the remains of an ancient fort? Something damaged in wartime? Perhaps there are pagan rituals involved? Unfortunately, the true story of the erection of the tower is both more simple and more prosaic. It was built in 1897 by John Stewart McCaig, a local banker, who planned it as a kind of late Victorian job-creation scheme. His idea was to provide work for the needy in the short term, and glory for the McCaigs in the end, for one of his notions was to place a series of statues in those windows commemorating his ancestors. By the time he died he had made the poor less poor by about £5000 – and his reward was to have his endeavour renamed 'McCaig's Folly'.

Oban, Argyll, Strathclyde ▷

As recently as the middle of the nineteenth century Oban could be described as a village; today, having expanded rapidly over the course of the past century and more, it is often called the Charing Cross of the Highlands. As that appellation suggests, the town is more of a gateway than a destination in itself, although it is also popular with holidaymakers and day trippers. From Oban you strike out for the Hebridean islands: Mull, Coll and Tiree, Colonsay and Oronsay ... and day and night Oban harbour is busy with fishing boats unloading their catches. The shelter offered to the bracket-shaped bay – Oban's name derives from the Gaelic for a bay – by the island of Kerrera (in the middle distance, dusted by clouds) makes Oban a convenient yachting port. In the background of this picture, finely delineated on a calm sea, almost seeming to be afloat, are the hills of Mull. What appear to be three islands fronting it are in fact peninsulas, between which are Lochs Don, Spelve and Buie.

◁ **Iona,** Argyll, Strathclyde

A mere three miles long by one and a half wide – composed of Torridonian sandstone, curiously unrelated geologically to neighbouring Mull – Iona is richer in Christian association than any other Scottish island. In AD 563 St Columba left Ireland with twelve companions to come here and found a monastery, and from that base he and his disciples embarked on missions to convert the natives of the lands that have since come to be known as Scotland. The sacred building along the central path on the island is the nunnery, built around 1200. Iona is only about ten minutes' sailing from Fionnphort on Mull, and a ferry runs back and forth at frequent intervals. Not this steamer, however, which is more likely to be returning from a further-flung excursion to Fingal's Cave.

Iona Cathedral ▷

All of Iona's religious buildings were desecrated during the Reformation. Nearly all of the ancient Celtic crosses were destroyed then too, though a few remain and are on view near St Mary's Cathedral. It was in the last century, when the island was bought by the Duke of Argyll, that the cathedral was restored and re-roofed: the first service in its reconditioned interior took place in 1910. Half a million visitors spill off the ferries on to the island every year; when you have taken one yourself it is hard at first to understand how there can be any peace at all on a place as small as this – three miles by one and a half – as boatload follows boatload. But Iona knows more than we do and seems to hold a handful of peaceful spots constantly in reserve.

Luing, Argyll, Strathclyde

The population of this island (pronounced 'ling') is now only about 200, but before the slate quarries closed down in 1965 it must have been higher. Today it is a lobster-fishing centre, with one of Britain's largest lobster ponds at nearby Eilean Fraoch. Luing has the unusual advantage – if advantage it may be called – of being a remote island which is easily accessible by road. The Clachan Bridge connects the island of Seil to the mainland, and then another links Seil and Luing – this being commonly known as the 'bridge over the Atlantic'. Here we look at Cullipool, Luing's main village, and a little lighthouse isle. We must assume that these yachts know where they are going, because once they pass through the Sound of Luing they will find themselves in the turbulent strait of Corryvreckan.

Corryvreckan, Argyll, Strathclyde

The infamous Corryvreckan whirlpool is a brew whipped up between the isles of Jura and Scarba, where the westward stream running through the Gulf of Corryvreckan into the Atlantic meets the eastward-running eddy over rough ground. In rough weather it is deadly, in calm weather merely dangerous. The turbulence creates the sound of boiling water, which is audible five miles away on Luing and which has produced the rhyme:

> Scarba's tortured shore
> Answers Corryvreckan's roar.

Jura still has people, but Scarba is the preserve of sheep and cattle.

Seil and Easdale, Argyll, Strathclyde ▷

The quarrying of slate began on these islands well over 300 years ago, and for most of that time held its place as the main industry of the area. At the beginning of this century 352 people were employed in the quarries hereabouts; by 1950 it was 37, and today it is nil: the last quarry – at Balvicar on Seil – closed down in 1965. Slates from these quarries contributed to the re-roofing of Iona Cathedral, but the eventual dearth of resources was not the only reason for their demise – high prices and declining demand for slate also played their parts. The industry has left its teethmarks everywhere on these islands off the coast near Oban. In November 1881 at Ellanbeich on Seil (only a corner of which is visible in this picture) the sea wall caved in under pressure from a high tide and the quarry was flooded; and, as the picture shows, others have followed suit.

◁ **Jura,** Argyll, Strathclyde

Some facts and figures help to suggest the character of life on Jura: the island is twenty-eight miles long by eight wide, has 5000 red deer and some goats but only 200 people and a single road, twenty-three miles long. The other half of the island, facing west, is uninhabited, trackless bog, difficult to cross. Some of its raised beaches are 100 feet above sea level, but they are almost exclusively the property of seabirds. Here we have a fine view of the Paps of Jura – Beinn a Chaolais, Beinn an Oir and Beinn Shiantaidh – each rising to more than 2000 feet. Jura has a place in English literary history: it was here that George Orwell wrote *Nineteen Eighty-Four.*

▽ **Port Ellen,** Islay, Argyll, Strathclyde

The island of Islay's prosperity derives from whisky: roughly four million gallons proof are produced here each year, and distilling employs about 200 people. At one time the islanders were rewarded with duty free Scotch themselves, with unfortunate results. Drunk with due care and attention, however, Islay malts are among the nation's finest, including the peaty Laphroig (pronounced 'Lafroyg'), to some the best of all.

△ Loch Craignish,
Argyll, Strathclyde

Lochranza, △
Island of Arran, Bute, Strathclyde

Loch Stornoway,
Argyll, Strathclyde ▷

Roughly twenty islands compose the constellation in and around Craignish, bounded by the tongue of Craignish on the west and the unapproachable coastline of the Kilmartin district on the east. Eilean Mhic Chrion, Eilean Righ, Eilean na Nighinn – none of these small islands is inhabited now, but some of them have jetties and forts to prove that people once struggled to make a living here. They still do so on the mainland, where the road stops before reaching Craignish Point, offering a fine view across to Scarba and Jura.

Together with the Island of Bute (Rothesay), the Cumbraes and a handful of smaller islands, Arran forms the shire of Bute: the only insular county in Scotland apart from Orkney and Shetland. It is fair to say that of the three holiday resorts, Arran, with an area of 165 square miles, has been voted the most scenically attractive. Lochranza is on its northwest tip. The plateau beyond the scatter of houses was formerly the bed of the loch itself, which used to drive in a mile or so further than at present, before relief from glacial weight caused the raised beach. Long after, Robert the Bruce stayed in the castle, to begin his campaign for Scotland's independence in the thirteenth and fourteenth centuries.

Not, as the name might suggest, situated in the island of Lewis in the Outer Hebrides, but in Knapdale, Loch Stornoway is barely deserving of the title of loch at all. It is little more than a sandy bay on the west of the tongue which droops into the Atlantic Ocean. The loch and the coast are seldom visited, though they are hardly remote, perhaps because the road which passes them winds in a circle back round the Lochgilphead, and so does not actually go anywhere. Here we look over to Jura and find a herd of cattle, confident of there being no bathers and undisturbed by the monster in the sky, cooling their ankles and making the most of the sunshine.

◁ **Island of Bute**, Bute, Strathclyde

If you were to ask a Glaswegian to tell you about the Island of Bute, they would either laugh or else ask what on earth you were talking about. For this island is concentrated on its eastern port and major holiday resort, Rothesay and by that name it is known throughout Scotland. The island (population 8000) has a deep history – its circular castle, for example, visible to the left, was begun in the eleventh century – but today Rothesay means putting greens and rowing boats and amusement arcades; and, of course, it means the steamer from Wemys Bay. Formerly Bute supplied agricultural produce to the mainland; now it depends mainly on tourism.

▽ **Tarbert**, Argyll, Strathclyde

On the east side of the isthmus which keeps West Loch Tarbert from Loch Fyne is the pretty fishing village of Tarbert (the name itself means an isthmus). In the eleventh century, Magnus Barfud, son of King Olaf of Norway, dragged his galley across the mile-wide isthmus; by rights set down in a treaty which had assigned him all the land he could circumnavigate, Knapdale therefore became his. The dodge of rolling boats on logs across the isthmus – to save a long and dangerous journey round the Mull of Kintyre – was common among Scottish fishermen, until in 1801 the opening of Crinan Canal, just north of here, made it unnecessary.

△ **Gigha Island,** Argyll, Strathclyde

Speculation continues concerning the derivation of the name Gigha (pronounced 'gee-a', with a hard 'g'), but one suggestion is that it comes from old Norse and means 'Island of God'. To discover for yourself if this is appropriate means taking the ferry from the Kintyre mainland across the Sound of Gigha to the six-mile-long island, which from this angle, looking south, resembles the map of Scotland itself. Although the sea is audible everywhere you turn on Gigha, those members of the 200-strong population who used to make a living from commercial fishing have had to look to the island's dozen or so farms, or elsewhere, since the fishing stopped. But the lime-free loam is fertile and the climate comparatively mild. The gardens of Achamore House have some rare plants, including several sub-tropical varieties, and are open to the public in summer. Like other islands nearby, Gigha is MacNeill territory, though they had to fight hard with the Macleans in the sixteenth century to prove it.

The Cumbraes, Bute, Strathclyde △

A local minister in the early nineteenth century, the Reverend James Adams, used to offer a prayer every Sunday in church for Great Cumbrae and Little Cumbrae 'and the adjacent islands of Great Britain and Ireland'. And rightly so, for the atmosphere of these two popular islands in the Firth of Clyde is quite their own. Our picture, showing Little Cumbrae in the foreground, reverses the true order of size. In popular parlance, Great Cumbrae is called after its only town, Millport. Before the Costa Brava was discovered by Glaswegians in the 1960s, the Costa Clyde was their favourite holiday playground, and Millport was often chosen for its island air and sandy bay, visible here beyond the tip of Little Cumbrae. Accessible from the town of Largs, in the background, it has a ring road which is perfect for cycling. Little Cumbrae has no sizeable settlements, only a farm, a large private house, and a disused lighthouse, and it is belted by a raised beach.

Holy Island, Bute, Strathclyde ▷

Until 1830 this island was called Lamlash, which is now the name of the town on the Island of Arran which it faces. Before that it was Eilean Molaise, after St Mo Las, the seventh-century Columban monk who lived here, supposedly until he reached the age of 120. There are scattered dwellings on the two-mile-long hump still, including the lighthouse to the foreground here; but the goats now have Holy Island to themselves, apart from the amateur mountaineers who by motor or elbow grease strike out to climb its 1000-foot peak.

◁ **Dunoon,** Argyll, Strathclyde

'A busy watering place' used to be the polite way of describing resorts like Dunoon, accessible across the Firth of Clyde by ferry from Gourock. An ancient seat of Scottish royalty (traces of its thirteenth-century castle can still be seen), Dunoon succeeded in remaining a village until the Victorians popularized the practice of going on holidays to the seaside. It is hard to imagine now that when the first batches of well-provisioned holidaymakers from Glasgow arrived it was to discover that only the local minister spoke English. Just beyond the town, under the Kilmun Hill, can be seen the waters of Holy Loch, named after the shipwreck of a vessel bound for Glasgow with a load of earth for its cathedral. It is now an American naval base, and the sailors' presence in town on a Saturday night ensures that, as a slightly different kind of watering place, it stays busy.

Yachts, Inverkip, Firth of Clyde ▷

Parachutists in distress? A pair of brightly coloured beachballs? This pair, on the Firth of Clyde near the old smugglers' haunt of Inverkip, are making the most of a powerful wind which will be driving bathers to distraction on the beach at Dunoon across the water.

Greenock and Port Glasgow,
Renfrewshire, Strathclyde

In the Clyde estuary in the west of Scotland, Port Glasgow (once but no longer what its name suggests), Greenock and Gourock form an almost continuous seven-mile-long urban and industrial strip, with the emphasis, of course, on the shipbuilding industry (although it is constantly in danger). Their combined population is over 100,000, two-thirds of which belongs to Greenock (*right*). Established as a port in the seventeenth century, Greenock quickly rose in importance so that by the end of that century half of all ships on the Clyde sailed from here, though no sea-going creature was actually created at Greenock until 1760. The first dock suitable for large vessels at Port Glagow was constructed two years later to a design by James Watt – born, conveniently, in Greenock in 1736. He is now commemorated by a monument, a museum, a scientific library and a dock. The town's other famous son is of a different shade of respectability: Captain Kidd the pirate lives on by reputation only.

The picture shows the extensive industrial vista of Greenock from the west end of the town (with, in the foreground, the sixteenth-century church containing windows by Morris, Rossetti and Burne-Jones). The left-hand picture shows a ship in the making, confirming that Port Glasgow is still in business.

Balloch, Dunbartonshire, Strathclyde

Every Scot has his or her personal choice for the 'gateway to the Highlands' and I suppose that Balloch, where the Glasgow train deposits weekenders on the road to Loch Lomondside, qualifies as mine. The River Leven, which begins at the loch just half a mile from here, has a course of only five miles, through a valley dark with industry, before opening into the Clyde at Dumbarton. The novelist Tobias Smollett, author of *Humphrey Clinker* and other novels, was born nearby in 1721. The pleasure craft below are probably about to make the trip to Loch Lomond, whether by motor, sail or oar.

Balmaha, Loch Lomond, Stirlingshire, Strathclyde ▷

Once the first stopping place of the many paddle steamers cruising up Loch Lomond, Balmaha is situated on the south-east side of the loch, less accessible than the west side, which takes the road going north from Glasgow. As the evidence of buses, cars and small pleasure craft in this picture proves, it is highly popular with tourists nonetheless. The sailors may head for any one of several tiny islands in the loch – Inchmurrin, perhaps, or Inchcailloch, which both have ancient ruins – or maybe in search of refreshment from the inn at Rowardennan, the destination of the road branching off to the left in our picture. The last paddle boat to be built in the country, *Maid of the Loch*, still travels up Loch Lomond, stopping first at Balmaha.

Loch Lomond, Stirlingshire, Strathclyde

Up here you can believe – if only for an instant – that the world is perfect. Loch Lomond will always hold fast to its reputation as Scotland's most picturesque loch, and at times can get away with it. There is no questioning its other claim to fame, however, that it is Britain's largest inland water: twenty-four miles long by five at the widest point – just here, as it happens. It may seem curious at first that the city of dreadful night, Glasgow, is almost within walking distance, just beyond the Campsie Hills which can be seen in the distance; but reflection suggests that it is its proximity to the big city which has gained this loch its reputation.

◁ Glasgow, Strathclyde

One suggested derivation of the name of Glasgow is the Celtic *glas cu*, meaning 'dear green place'; if the city no longer lives up to such a description, then Glasgow has in many ways been its own worst enemy. Once, the second city of the Empire was famous for the tobacco trade, then for shipbuilding; nowadays its public image is more likely to be a reflection of the violent acts certain members of the public commit against each other – usually known as hooliganism – or else the violent acts committed against the public by the town council – usually known as housing estates, motorways and flyovers. Networks of streets were swept away in the sixties and seventies to make way for these, but in many places, as a result of economic hardship or just bad planning, nothing has replaced them, and a portion of land which once was the base of a community is now a wasteland. Finally, it seems that word from beneath has got to the top: the verdict is 'No'. But Glasgow is like an old suit of clothes: if to the outsider it appears shabby, to the possessor it is irreplaceable.

Hillington, Renfrewshire, Strathclyde ▷

Four miles from the centre of Glasgow, Hillington was established in 1938 as the first industrial estate in Scotland. By the end of that year it had seventy tenants, and steady expansion ever since has allowed it to keep its position as the largest estate of its kind in the country. Today 170 of the 250 units are occupied and a total of 8000 people are employed on site in units varying in size from 150 to 100,000 square feet. Its success is no doubt due to a number of factors, including its position between the two thoroughfares of Glasgow and Greenock, and its nearness to airport, railway line and the Clyde, seen sneaking past in the top right corner. In 1983, incidentally, for the first time in 140 years, salmon were seen (and caught) in the River Clyde.

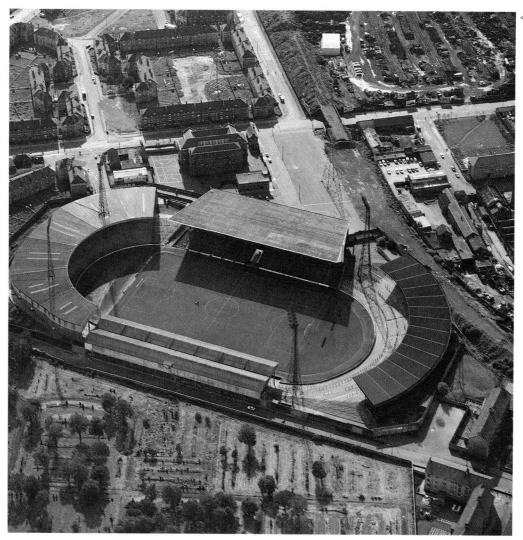

◁ Glasgow Celtic football ground

Of the three great Glasgow football clubs, Celtic was the last to be founded, coming two years after Rangers in 1874. (Queen's Park was first, in 1867, and today is the only amateur club in British senior football.) For all its fearsome reputation, a Celtic versus Rangers football match, with 70,000 fans thundering encouragement and disapproval all together, is one of Glasgow's great spectacles. Celtic occupy a special place in British football history: in 1967, under the management of Jock Stein, they became the first British club to win the European Cup, defeating the mighty Inter Milan by two goals to one in Lisbon. Even Rangers supporters cheered that night. Celtic Park (known locally as Parkhead, after the district in which it is situated) was built in 1893. The surrounding slums suggest one possible reason why the sight of green and white hoops on a Saturday afternoon retains a special glamour for thousands. Here the turf is being rolled in preparation for the next match.

George Square, Glasgow ▷

The largest open space in central Glasgow, George Square, laid out in 1781 and named after George III, may be considered the centre of the city itself. In 1837 it was crowned by Glasgow's tribute to the great Edinburgh novelist, Sir Walter Scott: an eighty-foot-high Doric column surmounted by a statue – the first to be raised to Scott. Around him, closer to ground level, are other immortals, including Burns, Watt, Livingstone and Peel. It is a traditional treat for Glaswegian children to be taken to see 'the statues' for the first time. On the right hand side, to the east, are the buildings of the City Chambers, built in 1883–8 by William Young in Italian Renaissance style. Backing away at the top left of the square is Queen Street Station, and its track, running to the north and east of the country, can be seen disappearing through the tunnel behind it.

Cumbernauld, Lanarkshire, Strathclyde

The concept of the 'New Town' travelled a long, arduous road between the day when James Craig presented his plans to the Edinburgh Town Council in 1768 and the passing of the New Towns Acts by a Labour Government in 1946. In Scotland, the Act was quickly followed by the designation of East Kilbride as the site of the nation's first new town. There is no doubt that something had to be done to ease overcrowding in Glasgow's slum districts and, on the whole, the new towns seem to have attracted more advocates than the faceless, barrack-like housing estates such as Easterhouse and Castlemilk. Few ever had the audacity to claim that the idea had been a total success, however, and in 1976 a sad event occurred when the first tenants of the new town of Stonehouse in Lanarkshire accepted their keys, only to be informed two days later that the project had been abandoned – and with it, symbolically, went the hope which had been invested in new towns. Cumbernauld was begun in 1956 (leading architect, L. Hugh Wilson) with a target population of 70,000. With good shopping centres and its own theatre, it is better served than some inner-city areas. These two pictures of the Kildrum district give an impression of the schematic layout, and of the ideal of keeping housing varied, compact and close to roads and green areas, even if little could grow in the spaces in between.

◁ **Hamilton,** Lanarkshire, Strathclyde

△ **Fairground,** Hamilton

Hamilton was made a royal burgh in 1548, and the history of the town includes many notable incidents, but modern Hamilton owes its existence to coal-mining, which until after the Second World War was its major industry – and, of course, the main source of employment. By the late forties, however, the pits were closing and miners' sons learned to make carpets, metal castings, bricks and other products. This centripetal housing development on the left bank of the Clyde (just visible at the top of the photograph) makes it hard to avoid the feeling that from time to time little happens in Hamilton.

For entertainment purposes, Hamilton is best known for its racecourse, which hosts approximately fifteen meetings every year during the flat season. But this cheerfully coloured fairground is more likely to draw the younger Hamiltonians. Judging by the number of lorries and vans used to form the surrounding barricades, it employs quite a number of administrators and helpers.

◁ Ravenscraig,
Motherwell, Lanarkshire, Strathclyde

Although there have been settlements here since at least Roman times, Motherwell's current outfit was tailored to fit the coal and iron industries which developed during the last century and the present one. Most of the pits are closed now, though, and the iron works have been converted to produce steel. At Ravenscraig – seen here at full blast on the kind of dusky afternoon which seems to be more common in places like Motherwell than elsewhere – steel is manufactured and rolled. Until recently the works was a success, but discussions of the role it is to play in the British steel industry of the eighties have a less cheerful tone about them.

Ardrossan, Ayrshire, Strathclyde ▷

Ardrossan was formally laid out in 1806 on a plan by Peter Nicholson, and its harbour dates from about forty years later, having had to wait until the railway came from Glasgow before it could be completed. It extends over seventeen acres, and this picture, taken at a giddy angle, makes its function as a port quite plain. However, the town is also a resort visited for its own sake in summer by holidaymakers, and is aided in this respect by being linked to the seaside town of Saltcoats less than a mile to the south. One of these boats is about to depart, possibly for the Isle of Man, or for Arran, just across the Firth of Clyde.

◁ **Butlin's Holiday Camp,**
Ayr, Ayrshire, Strathclyde

If you were to mistake it for a wartime camp it wouldn't be at all surprising, for that is what it was. The Butlin's holiday camp four miles from the town of Ayr was built by Billy Butlin's men in 1941, and opened in the guise of a naval training station. Two years after the end of the war the conversions needed to accommodate holidaymakers were completed, and Butlin's offered board and lodging to 3000 fun-seekers – with the famous bait that the fun was free.

△ **Ayr,** Ayrshire, Strathclyde

The modern fame of this 'ancient city by an ancient sea' is as a holiday resort on the Firth of Clyde. Come the height of summer, the sprinkling of bathers seen here braving the waters will be augmented by families on a fortnight's holiday and also by day-trippers from Glasgow, just an hour's journey away. Ayr is one of Scotland's oldest royal burghs, having gained its charter in 1202. In 1759 Robert Burns was born in the village of Alloway, just a mile or two behind us. His most famous poem about Ayr is a dialogue between the auld brig and the new brig, which was built in 1788. Unperturbed by the snooty comments of the new brig, the auld brig prophesies that he will 'be a Brig when you're a shapeless cairn'. A century later he was proved correct, when the new brig was swept away during floods.

◁ Ailsa Craig, Ayrshire, Strathclyde

One travel writer displayed typical Scottish pride, if not ingenuity, by writing that Ailsa Craig was from a certain angle a perfect pyramid, 'with this advantage over the pyramids of Egypt, that it is twice their height'. Ailsa Craig, the fairy rock, Paddy's Milestone (so called because of its position halfway between Glasgow and Belfast), is a volcanic lump ten miles off the coast of Girvan, 1100 feet high. It belongs in Scotland all right, in the parish of Dailly. The memory bank which every Scottish adult reserves for holidays on the Clyde is haunted by it ('Where *is* Ailsa Craig, again?'). It houses a ruined castle and a lighthouse, is riddled with rabbit warrens and shrieking with gulls, and is also a quarry for a special kind of granite (ailsite) used for best quality curling stones.

Culzean Castle, Ayrshire, Strathclyde ▷

Situated above the bay from which it takes its name, Culzean Castle (pronounced Cull-ain) was built for the Earl of Cassillis (Kennedy family) by Robert Adam, the greatest architect Scotland has produced, between 1777 and the year of his death, 1792. Culzean is a castle built long after the age of castles, and it was never intended to withstand military might. Its *raison d'être*, therefore, is romance. As its many visitors will testify (the castle and its grounds were handed over to the nation by the Marquess of Ailsa in 1945) the idea was well put into practice. Culzean combines Gothic and Classical styles, being castellated on the outside but with the grandeur of a Georgian interior. The bridges, the carefully studied 'ruins', the turrets and parapets, the sea on one side and fertile Ayrshire fields on the others, combine to make it the 'dream castle' the Earl was hoping for, and it is Adam's most spectacular creation in his native land.

Mull of Galloway,
Wigtonshire, Dumfries and Galloway

The Rhinns of Galloway project like an axe-head from the south-west corner of Scotland; this long stretch of land is not to be confused with the mull of the same name, only its southern tip, across which we look here. A rugged coastline with small beaches and natural harbours stretches back to the neck of land upon which sits Stranraer, which connects the Rhinns to the main body of the country. Where the lighthouse stands the cliffs are 270 feet high, and stay over 200 for much of the way back. Just below the last farmstead is St Medan's Cave which has a chapel built into it; the Marquess of Bute excavated it in 1872 and immediately regretted doing so, when a crowd of Protestants from Stranraer seized the relics and threw the lot into the sea. (It may have had something to do with the fact that on a clear day Ireland is perfectly visible from here.)

150

◁ Dumfries,
Dumfriesshire, Dumfries and Galloway

Although there are traces of Dark Ages settlement, as far as history is concerned Dumfries struggled into being in the twelfth century when William the Lion made it a royal burgh. Ever since, it has been developing and changing on loops of the River Nith, five miles from its estuary in the Solway Firth. Dumfries is called 'Queen of the South' (as is the local football team), for being the main commercial centre in the south of Scotland. The town paid for that distinction too, like all Border towns and villages, in the Middle Ages. In calmer times, Dumfries is perhaps best known for the association with Robert Burns, who worked as an exciseman here from 1791 until his death five years later. Little of the town that Burns knew survives today, but the central riverfront still has an exciting busy-ness about it, day and night.

Lowther Hill, Lanarkshire, Strathclyde ▷

Lowther Hill is one of the highest (2378 feet) of the range of hills which is sometimes named after it, and sometimes after the village of Leadhills nearby (second highest in Scotland). In 1948 it was chosen for obvious reasons to be the base of a long-range radar station built by the Ministry of Civil Aviation. The main employment in the parish of Wanlockhead used to be lead-mining, but since the mines closed local men have had to look elsewhere. This giant tee with two golf balls provides work for no more than a handful.

153

◁ Morton Castle,
Dumfriesshire, Dumfries and Galloway

The builders of medieval castles must have chosen their sites for beauty as well as inviolability, and it is a source of amazement to us today how many, after 700–800 years, offer an impression similar to that experienced by their first beholders. No doubt things have changed a little more than one might suspect around Morton Loch, but there is still little in view that is man-made. This castle was built in the mid-thirteenth century on a steep promontory overlooking the loch which gives it its name. It is on the site of an earlier structure of which we know little, except that it was possibly the seat of Dunegal, Lord of Nithsadale, a kingdom which covered present day Nithsdale and Clydesdale.

Drumlanrig Castle,
Dumfriesshire, Dumfries and Galloway ▷

Drumlanrig, home of the Duke of Buccleuch, was built in pink sandstone in the late seventeenth century, probably by James Mylne. Famous artists represented within include Holbein, Rowlandson, Murillo and Rembrandt. Signatories in the visitors' book include Charles Edward Stuart, the Young Pretender, who lodged here for a night during the last days of his doomed adventure. Only a fraction of the 177,700 acre estate is visible, but sufficient to convey the flavour.

▽ Berwick-upon-Tweed,
Northumberland

Once Scotland's richest and most powerful burgh, Berwick is now settled across the border in Northumberland – leaving behind the Scottish shire of Berwick whose regent county town (for the meantime anyway) is Duns. Berwick is both an English and a Scottish town, however, and deserves its place in this book. During the Middle Ages it was bounced backwards and forwards, like many border towns and villages, between Scotland and England, being settled in the latter in 1482. Today Berwick is the headquarters of a Scottish regiment, the Queen's Own Borderers; it receives its supply of gas from England but its electricity from Scotland; its boy scouts are English but its girl guides Scottish; and its football team plays in the Scottish professional divisions. Moreover, it is commonly (though of course mistakenly) thought by travellers to be the point at which they leave Scotland behind and enter English territory, whereas the border is a few miles to the north. But look along the Tweed away from its mouth, beyond the Whiteadder tributary: the point where the serpent's tail comes to an end is Scotland.

◁ Langholm,
Dumfriesshire, Dumfries and Galloway

'Gathering hines in the Langfall; going through the fields of Baggara hedged in honeysuckle and wild roses, through knee-deep meadow-sweet to the Scrog Nut Wood and gathering the nuts or crab-apples there . . .' Langholm sprouts at the point where the Esk, Ewes and Wauchope waters meet, and is encircled by five glens. It is the birthplace of two great Scots, Thomas Telford and Christopher Murray Grieve (Hugh MacDiarmid) who wrote the above lines. By a happy coincidence, MacDiarmid was born in a house below a library left to the town by Telford, and claimed to have read every one of its 20,000 books by the age of fourteen. Here we look across the Esk on to the main street of the town: MacDiarmid's birthplace is in the building which terminates it. All Border towns hold an annual Common Riding, the ceremony whereby the people enact their right of access to the common ground. Langholm's is one of the most elaborate festivals, and also one of the oldest, having been established in 1759.

INDEX

Numbers in *italics* refer to illustrations